P9-EDY-832

FRENCH
FAMILY COOKING

Audrey Ellis

Spring Books

London · New York · Sydney · Toronto

CONTENTS

Cover photograph by James Jackson
Photography by Christian Délu
Line drawings by Rosemary Aldridge

First published in 1974 by
The Hamlyn Publishing Group Limited

This edition published in 1983 by
Spring Books
Astronaut House, Feltham, Middlesex, England

ISBN 0 600 38532 9

Printed in Hong Kong

USEFUL FACTS AND FIGURES

NOTE ON METRICATION

In this book quantities have been given in both metric and Imperial measures. Exact conversion from Imperial to metric measures does not usually give very convenient working quantities and so for greater convenience we have rounded off metric measures into units of 25 grammes. The table below shows recommended equivalents.

Ounces/fluid ounces	Approx. g. and ml. to nearest whole figure	Recommended conversion to nearest unit of 25
1	28	25
2	57	50
3	85	75
4	113	100
5 ($\frac{1}{4}$ pint)	142	150
6	170	175
7	198	200
8 ($\frac{1}{2}$ lb.)	226	225
9	255	250
10 ($\frac{1}{2}$ pint)	283	275
11	311	300
12	340	350
13	368	375
14	396	400
15 ($\frac{3}{4}$ pint)	428	425
16 (1 lb.)	456	450
17	484	475
18	512	500
19	541	550
20 (1 pint)	569	575

Note When converting quantities over 20 oz. first add the appropriate figures in the centre column, *then* adjust to the nearest unit of 25. As a general guide, 1 kg. (1000 g.) equals 2·2 lb. or about 2 lb. 3 oz.; 1 litre (1000 ml.) equals 1·76 pints or almost exactly 1$\frac{3}{4}$ pints.

This method of conversion gives good results in nearly all recipes. However, where the proportion between liquids and solids is critical, for example in baking recipes, a more accurate conversion is necessary to preserve the exact proportions of the recipe. In these cases we have used a conversion to the nearest 5 grammes.

Liquid measures

The millilitre is a very small unit of measurement and we felt that to use decilitres (units of 100 ml.) would be less cumbersome. In most cases it is perfectly satisfactory to round off the exact millilitre conversion to the nearest decilitre, except for $\frac{1}{4}$ pint; thus $\frac{1}{4}$ pint (142 ml.) is 1$\frac{1}{2}$ dl.,

$\frac{1}{2}$ pint (283 ml.) is 3 dl., $\frac{3}{4}$ pint (428 ml.) is 4 dl., and 1 pint (569 ml.) is 6 dl. For quantities over 1 pint we have used litres and fractions of a litre. Where the exact proportions are critical we have used the millilitre conversion.

Note At present cans normally show the exact metric conversion of the Imperial weight of the contents and we have followed this practice when giving can sizes.

NOTES FOR AMERICAN USERS

In the recipes in this book quantities are given in American standard cup and spoon measures as well as Imperial and metric measures. The list below gives some American equivalents or substitutes for terms used in the book.

BRITISH	AMERICAN
basin	bowl
biscuit cutter	cookie cutter
cake tin	cake pan
celeriac	celery root
chicory	Belgian endive
clotted cream	see note below
cream	see note below
cream cheese	see note below
endive	curly endive or chicory
fillet	tenderloin
flan tin/ring	pie pan
frying pan	skillet
greaseproof paper	wax paper
kitchen paper	paper towels
liquidiser	blender
mince	grind
muslin	cheesecloth
patty tins	muffin pans
piping bag	pastry bag
shallow flan tin	layer cake pan
whisk	beat/whip

Cream

In France all cream is heavy and can be whipped; it will hold its shape when thin cream, egg white or liquid is added. If a recipe calls for cream to which you add another ingredient then use heavy cream, otherwise you can use heavy or whipping cream. In the recipe on page 72 for galette, clotted cream is called for. This is made by slowly heating the cream skimmed from scalded milk to not more than 150°F. Otherwise, use very thick heavy cream.

Cream cheese

Petit-suisse is fresh cream cheese. You may use another unsalted cream cheese instead if you cannot obtain this sort. Elsewhere when cream cheese is called for, e.g., demi-sel, use an ordinary cream cheese such as Philadelphia.

Note All recipes in this book, unless otherwise indicated, serve an average-sized family.

INTRODUCTION

This is a highly individual book. I do not claim that I have made a lifelong study of French cooking. I merely state that my grandfather was a Frenchman; he bequeathed me, as well as flashing black eyes and a volatile temperament, an enormous enjoyment of, and veneration for, good food cooked in the French manner.

Fortunately he also endowed me with a *parenté* of innumerable kind and hospitable aunts, uncles and cousins. Although I am the only cookery writer in the family, I am not the only dedicated cook. Many relatives, both near and dear and far distant, have contributed their admirable recipes to this book. It does not pretend to initiate readers into the mysteries of *haute cuisine*, but merely to introduce them to the French *cuisine familiale* – less elaborate but infinitely satisfying, and certainly more practical for the busy housewives of other lands to imitate.

The glory of French cooking is its immense scope, embracing great regional variations in climate, in tastes and in food available. Most of my recipes have a flavour of the north-west, a region rich in homely dishes made with apples, eggs, bacon, cream, and fish from a northern sea comparable to our own. There are others, more picturesque, from the Midi, and my grandfather's favourite birthday dinner from Alsace; but none, I hope, to leave the reader wistful because the cost would be prohibitive or the ingredients unobtainable.

That supreme artist, the French chef, is a master of countless cookery techniques. Not every French housewife has the time or inclination to follow all his precepts, but even in the humblest home cooking ranks as an art, not a chore. *Maman* gives her time and effort to it ungrudgingly, because every mouthful of food is savoured, enjoyed, and commented on, by the family.

But she does move with the times. The cookery cards from a great national magazine, which innumerable Frenchwomen cut out and keep, unashamedly advise the use of bought frozen puff pastry, and not one of my relatives still makes her own puff paste. I have given no recipe for it, and a few other 'classics' are omitted for the same reason. Other dishes are left out because, like certain wines, they do not travel well. A true *bouillabaisse* seems to need Mediterranean fish, and experiments with flour available here in making Breton *crêpes de sarrasin* have been disappointing. If you search for recipes using *cèpes* and *morilles* in vain it is for the same reason. Faced with making a choice among hundreds of family favourites, I left them out. The remainder were mouth-watering enough.

French cooking seems adventurous to us because of the liberal use of wine, even of spirits, and certainly of herbs and garlic. Garlic is fortunately an optional extra which can be toned down to a whisper if preferred. Wine is not cheap, but the glorious results are worth every drop. Where long, slow cooking can be speeded up without impairing the nature of the dish I have altered the method a little, but French cooks are not impatient and are prodigal in their attentions to finishing touches, such as the presentation of vegetables. They are careful shoppers, who comb the market stalls to find the firmest tomatoes, the ripest aubergines.

Some dishes you may consider somewhat rich and highly seasoned, and this is true. Every Frenchman has a lifelong love affair with his liver; worries over it, abuses it, nurses it through innumerable *'crises de foie'*. Usually if temporary starvation and a well-brewed *infusion* fail to arrange matters, a diet of boiled rice and leek soup for two days succeeds. Plain boiled rice is unexciting, but a French leek soup is almost worth the crisis. My French soul is anguished when I hear children moan, 'No nasty greens, Mummy!' In France vegetables are worthy to be presented, savoured, and enjoyed *alone* in their own right.

Customs and habits connected with eating vary from country to country, and these seem particularly French. At family meals, wine is usually drunk in tumblers; the sight of wine glasses on the table often signals the appearance of guests. Bread, once cut into thick slices and piled into baskets, is broken apart; for some reason, cutting bread on one's own plate is wrong. The final insult to the hostess would be to add extra salt and pepper to any dish without tasting it first, as this presupposes she does not know how to season food. Bottled sauces and pickles, though they may be discreetly hidden in the kitchen cupboard, never appear on a dining table.

Maman does not deal out piled plates, although this would save washing up. The meat and vegetable dishes are handed round from person to person, each solemnly holding the platter for his neighbour to partake, and then circulated again for second helpings. When the end is in sight, everyone gets more and more polite, with cries of *'Sers-toi!' 'Mais non, sers-toi!'*, until the last delicious morsel has been taken. Extra vegetables, always put to a good use as hors-d'oeuvre, are usually prudently put aside in the kitchen before the serving dishes go round, as these tend to go on circulating until empty. One other custom, to my mind the most charming of all, is that of urging the family to the table by instructing the youngest child to sing this little rhyme:
>*'A table, à table, les grands et les petits;*
>*A table, à table, à tous bon appetit.'*

May I wish all my readers, both young and old, a good appetite to enjoy the dishes which please my own family.

Audrey Ellis

EATING THE FRENCH WAY

The French kitchen

Come into a typical French kitchen with me. You may be equally surprised to find utensils and pieces of equipment you would never think of using, and the total absence of others which are as dear to you as your own right hand.

French cooks prefer to use exactly the right tool for each job and are not daunted by the fact that it may be as primitive as the pestle and mortar for pounding, or as highly specialised as a *mandoline* for fancy slicing.

Here is a list of a typical French housewife's *batterie de cuisine* with English equivalents of the names where these exist. But since French is the language of cookery, as it is of love, many French cookery terms and utensils have taken their place in foreign languages as of right.

List of equipment and utensils

1 Small wire whisk and larger balloon whisk for quickly beating up egg whites, whisking sauces to keep them smooth over heat, etc. The liquidiser or even a rotary beater are not considered part of the basic essentials.

2 Fluted flan rings and fluted flan cases (with false bottoms) in several sizes for all kinds of sweet and savoury tarts, and a *tourtière*, a deep tart tin.

3 A *moulin à légumes* for making purées of fruit and vegetables with a choice of grating discs.

4 Small pestle and mortar, plus a larger size if there is no electric blender, and a round-bladed *hachinette* for chopping herbs.

5 *Cocottes* and *ramequins* of china or earthenware for individual mousses, pâtés and egg dishes baked in the oven.

6 Salt mill for grinding *gros sel* or a salt box for rough kitchen salt. Pepper mills for grating white and black corns.

7 A selection of Sabatier knives, which, having steel blades, tend to discolour and need keeping clean as well as sharp. A large cook's knife for chopping, a short vegetable knife, a thin bladed carving knife and a very flexible palette knife are necessities. They need careful

storage to protect the fine cutting edges.

8 Most kitchens can boast a large hair or nylon sieve in a wooden frame for purées, a conical strainer or *chinois* for sauces, and several fine bowl sieves for sifting.

9 Graters would include one with various faces, the largest for grating cheese, the smallest for lemon zest, and a baby version for grating nutmeg.

10 China soufflé dishes in several sizes.

11 Two chopping boards, of which the smaller only is used for garlic and onion to prevent flavours mingling. (Garlic is rarely put through a press, but crushed with the back of a knife blade.) A marble slab is often used because the classic French method is to sieve flour into a heap on it, make a well in the centre and blend in the remaining ingredients rather than using a mixing bowl; a long wooden rolling pin is always well in view.

12 Some items to be found in any modern kitchen, including a French one, are: can opener, potato peeler, kitchen scissors, wooden spoons, slotted spoons, basting spoons, and measuring spoons and jugs. (French recipes very often refer to measurements by 'the glass' meaning about 6 fl. oz. (170 ml., $\frac{3}{4}$ cup), or an average wine glass, and 'soup spoons' and 'coffee spoons', roughly equivalent to our tablespoons and a small teaspoon.) The collection of forks always includes one carving fork with a really foolproof guard, and a large three-pronged cooking fork *à la diable*.

13 Terrines, both open oblong ones and oblong and oval ones with lids, are considered distinct from casseroles. The latter term can mean a huge saucepan with lid, a 1-pint (6-dl., 2½-cup) *cocotte* or anything in between in classic terra-cotta, earthenware (such as a *daubière*) or highly glazed ovenproof and flameproof ceramic. A *cocotte-minute* (pressure cooker) is used in many homes.

14 Pans would include a copper or stainless steel sauté pan, frying pan, set of saucepans, one small and one large omelette pan, a roasting tin (deep enough to be used as a *bain-marie*), and possibly a double boiler, fish kettle or steamer.

15 Mixing bowls are similar everywhere but the real French bowl still preferred for whisking egg whites to incredible bulk has a handle on one side and a rounded bottom so that you must hold it steady on a flat

surface with one hand while you whisk with the other.

16 As well as soufflé dishes and *moules à gelée*, for fruit jellies, what we call cake tins are also called moulds in French; most useful are *timbales*, *darioles*, *moules à manqué* and *moules à douille* (ring moulds).

17 Strong vegetable piping bags with plain and fancy tubes enable the French housewife to give a nice piped border to many entrées.

Comparative cookery terms and ingredients

Many basic cookery techniques have French names for which there is no translation – for example a *roux* which is a blend of fat and flour cooked only until very pale gold before adding liquid for a light coloured sauce, and cooked on to a rich nut brown for a dark sauce. An alternative liaison to thicken sauces is *beurre manié*, in which the uncooked blended flour and butter is stirred into the hot sauce almost at the end. Many more of these terms appear in this book.

Onions The more delicately flavoured shallot is often used in French cooking and large spring onions or blanched Spanish onion is a better substitute than a strongly flavoured home-grown variety. The use of garlic rarely, if ever, affects the finished texture of the dish so in many cases can be reduced in quantity or even omitted.

Mushrooms The French have a great variety of edible fungi, some very strongly flavoured and entirely different from the cultivated mushrooms of delicate flavour we can easily buy. For this reason I have avoided including

recipes which require a certain type of mushroom rarely available even in cans; and truffles I have left out on the grounds of expense, as they are too costly for the average family table.

Cream Only double cream is sold in France and is therefore given as an ingredient. Where this would make the dish very rich, or costly to make, the reader can substitute single cream if it does not have to be whipped until thick.

Oil and vinegar Olive oil is always used in French cooking where its delicate and distinctive flavour is essential. The more expensive variety, the first pressing, gives the most noticeable flavour of the olive itself. For frying and salad dressings, groundnut oil, *huile d'arachides*, is frequently used and for this corn oil is an acceptable substitute. Wine vinegar is much preferred in France to malt vinegar and tarragon vinegar imparts a faint flavour of the herb to many favourite dishes. In Normandy, where cider is a popular drink, an alternative is cider vinegar.

Herbs Since fresh herbs and home-dried herbs by the bunch are so readily available in French markets, the quantities allowed are usually much more generous than if one has recourse to jars of commercially dried herbs.

Le petit déjeuner
Breakfast

Breakfast is rarely a leisurely affair in French households since the working day starts extremely early and even a top executive expects to be in his office by eight in the morning. School children too leave home so early that they are inclined to gulp a hasty bowl of milky coffee and rush off just like *Papa*, clutching a *serviette* (a bulging briefcase of books), having dunked one buttered slice of bread in the coffee and buttered another one to eat *en route* to school. This bread would be cut on the cross, to make a larger slice, from a long *baguette*, or the richer *baguette viennoise*, in slices an inch thick. Some families prefer *ficelles* or *flûtes*, the very narrow loaves which are broken off into lengths of about six inches, being too thin to slice. Each person splits his portion lengthwise and sandwiches it together with butter and, if time permits, non-dunkers add *confiture*. Most *confiture* recipes turn out more runny than our jams and the proportion of pieces of fruit is rather disappointing. I have chased one strawberry round a large dish of jam intended for a family breakfast for six. Grown-ups drink stronger milky coffee in very large cups if not in bowls, and also enjoy *tartines trempées* unless foreign visitors are present. In more wealthy households, and on important occasions, there will be *croissants* for breakfast, fresh from the baker and so buttery that they are eaten just with jam or honey. In the home, coffee with chicory is still served because it is less *énervant* than pure coffee but if you pop into a *café* on your way to work for your breakfast, which (unless *Maman* is an early riser and prepared to slip down to the bakers before seven o'clock) may be your habit, you will ask for *un café complet* which means real coffee in a large cup with plenty of hot milk, rolls, butter and a croissant, perhaps even a tiny pot of jam or honey as well. *Brioches*, which are even more expensive than *croissants*, rarely appear on the family breakfast table, and are only eaten in better class hotels along with the many delightful shapes in which *petits pains* are still made. At home, if one wants rolls, they will be the traditional *baton* shape. Large loaves, suitable for sliced bread, toast and sandwiches, are made of *pain de mie* and the texture is rather dry and uninteresting. However, it must be said that they keep for 24 hours, which the classic type of French bread does not; it goes stale very quickly. That is why bread is baked and bought at least twice in every 24 hours in France and the previous day's bread is not very appetising for breakfast.

Various regions have their own shapes and varieties of bread. For instance, in Brittany every baker sells a *couronne*, a beautiful fancy round loaf, but in other regions the same bread would be baked in the form of a plait and called a *natte*. Really big families, especially in the country, have a huge loaf called a *boulot*, which weighs at least 4 lb. and can weigh as much as 8 lb. The shape of it is a sort of flattened cylinder.

Housewives in France would be astonished at the pride which housewives in other countries take in baking their own bread. Since there is so little factory baked bread and every baker is a craftsman who understands the vagaries of his own oven, it is unnecessary. Even tiny general stores in out-of-the-way places where there is no bakery put out a sign which says *station de pain*, which means that freshly baked bread is delivered there at least once a day.

Stale bread is not put out for the birds – it is used as a thickening agent in soups and stews, or dried off in the oven to form *biscottes*, a sort of rusk, and *croûtes*, for soup.

Le déjeuner
Lunch

As soon as the family is out of sight, *Maman* has to think about the mid-day meal because in France it really does take place at noon and that is why breakfast need not be a serious affair. Even today, the head of the household and the children almost always come home to lunch – the lunch-hour break extends to two hours to permit this – and in the southern regions where it is very hot for most of the year, shops are often closed from noon until four in the afternoon for the *sieste*.

The meal is composed of a minimum of three courses, starting with hors-d'oeuvre. Economical French women always include any vegetables left over from the previous night's meal, chilled and sprinkled with *vinaigrette*. In my family, more mushrooms than are required are often cooked in the evening and they are served masked with mayonnaise as part of the hors-d'oeuvre. Then comes the main dish, which is always substantial and accompanied by an appetite-quenching mountain of potatoes, rice or noodles – or a green vegetable. *Nouilles* are the only form of pasta enjoyed throughout France, although spaghetti is as popular in the Midi as it is in Italy. This will be followed by a salad. The cook will put a *vinaigrette* dressing in the bottom of the salad bowl and lay the well washed greenstuff on top and because it has been whirled dry in a *panier à salade* or patted dry in a tea-towel, it will remain crisp until the moment of service. One member of

the family is invited to turn the salad, to coat every leaf with dressing, and then it is handed round quickly before it has time to get limp. Each person has a *porte couteau*, a little resting place for knife and fork to the right of the plate, and as bread is eaten throughout the meal, the remains of each course are lovingly mopped up with a morsel of bread, so that the flavour of the preceding item does not mingle with the next, unless one wishes. The plate is often not changed right through from hors-d'oeuvre to salad.

If the main dish is a joint or grilled meat, the juices including the fat in which it was cooked are often not thickened, but poured into a sauceboat and served with it. There is a world of difference between our customary thickened gravy and a French sauce, which would never be made with coloured and seasoned cornflour, but on a roux basis, so the juices from the meat are often served in this way and used to moisten the green vegetable. If not, it would certainly be turned in butter before serving.

Now comes the cheese, which, contrary to our custom, is not served at the end of the meal. If red wine is being drunk, it will be finished up with the cheese before fruit or sweet arrive. Fresh fruit, rarely eaten between meals by the French, is a course in itself. Otherwise, the sweet is usually a fruit tart from the *pâtisserie*, since in France women prefer to leave the art of making delicate pastries to the *pâtissier*, expensive though this may be.

Red or white wine may be drunk with the meal, water for the children, or a local mineral water for the health conscious. Apart from the big milky cup of breakfast

coffee, children do not drink much milk although watered *grenadine*, a sweet strawberry-flavoured syrup, is a comparatively frequent treat. If guests are present, coffee will be served with a little *digestif* – a cognac or for the ladies *un liqueur d'anis*.

Le goûter

This meal is the closest any French family has to a snack, or our afternoon tea. It is usually served in households with school children or a member whose working hours do not fit into the accepted routine of breakfast at seven, lunch at noon, and dinner at eight. It used to be described as *le feef o'clock* by anglophiles, although more often served at four than at five, and is still considered an elegant way to entertain friends informally. Indian or China tea is served with sugar and lemon, and for older people a *tisane* or *infusion* of herbs, 'for the digestion'. Coffee is frequently served or a sparkling white wine, if possible champagne or another *vin mousseux*, with *sablés*, or other delicate home-baked biscuits. It has always been the custom in my family to serve *sablés* on a round plate, built up like a circular brick tower to a height of at least five layers, quite a feat as they break so easily.

Another favourite to offer guests for *le goûter* is a *brioche*, so often touchingly described in French recipes as *une belle brioche*, meaning a large one. One knows it has taken so much time and trouble to make, it seems a shame to cut into it. Slices are eaten plain, or with butter and jam by the really greedy.

A *tisane* is usually made by pouring boiling water over camomile, straining it off and drinking it unsweetened in a pretty teacup to make it more palatable. An *infusion* is stronger, and a *théière* keeps the brew hot for those who can face a second dose. Young girls are still firmly handed an *infusion* instead of the more fashionable aspirin for their headaches. Even in offices, there is a secretive sort of brewing ceremony of *tisanes*, about tea-time, and although much more coffee is drunk in France than in most other countries, more people eschew it entirely on the grounds that it is bad for their nerves, or that their digestions are too delicate to stand it. Instant coffee is not disdained, but is far from the rule. If your hostess offers *une petite tasse de café*, she means the real thing.

The children, of course, come home starving from school and are allowed to finish off the lunchtime bread in the form of *tartines*, rarely with butter, but liberally spread with honey or jam. It must be said that a crushed garlic clove mixed with butter is considered a socially acceptable substitute, but it certainly makes its presence felt if you travel in a crowded bus next to someone who has eaten it, later in the evening. *Maman* really prefers the children to finish up the bread as this ensures one of them will *faire les courses* – run her shopping errands including buying fresh bread. Shopping takes place with great verve in France between five and seven o'clock since the proprietors are reinvigorated after a long lunch break and a nap. Many people either shop on their way home from work or send the children with lists written on squared paper from their homework books. The reward is *vingt sous* to buy a *petit pain au chocolat*, or a *chausson aux pommes*.

Another charming French expression for a snack, served in a café at any hour, is a *casse-croûte*, literally no more than a broken crust, but really a French equivalent of the hamburger, such as *croque monsieur*, or more probably *un sandwich*, since this word has passed into the French language.

Le dîner

Dinner is either the culinary highlight of the day, or a lighter meal than lunch, according to the family's eating habits. If everyone comes home to lunch, the serious eating takes place then. The main dish will be roast, grilled or fried meat, alternating with fish and poultry, and the evening meal features an entrée or omelette, or a simple casserole. In any event, dinner always starts with soup. In the country, it would probably be the bouillon from a *pot-au-feu*, or a *garbure* – fresh vegetable soup, varied according to what is in season, cooked in stock, with a good nut of butter stirred into the tureen just as it comes to the table. Few town dwellers make stock nowadays. The handy little cube has superseded the stockpot simmering endlessly at the back of the stove. Modern cookers discourage stock-making in the towns of France as elsewhere, but the daily plateful of soup remains constant, assuaging the first pangs of appetite as economically as possible. Thrift is the essence of French cooking, so the artful cook makes the soup as delicious and as filling as possible and insists that it is all finished up. Then comes the entrée. It could be vegetables – asparagus, or globe artichokes. Melted butter or vinaigrette might be offered with either. Or it might be a pâté or an omelette.

The main dish follows, then a vegetable. If *Maman* is tired, there might be just a salad instead. The meal concludes with a home-made sweet, often *gâteau au riz*, or *au sémoule*, turned out of a pretty mould, or *crème caramel*. In hot weather you might have fresh fruit with *fromage blanc*, or a mousse. This usually means blancmange, but ambitious cooks lighten its texture with eggs and enrich it with cream, especially for guests.

Black coffee, not always served after lunch, always concludes the evening meal. Glasses for wine and water are provided for both the main meals of the day, the local *vin tiré*, or *vin ordinaire*, being liberally watered for the younger children if they have it at all; and at about the same age they get their introduction to black coffee in the form of a sugar lump dipped into *Papa*'s cup until it turns dark brown and begins to disintegrate. This is called *un canard*, and the young initiate is invited to open his or her 'beak' for the dripping delicacy, and then firmly advised to 'fly away', as a second one is not allowed. Baskets of bread are as liberally stacked for the evening meal as at lunchtime, and if no-one is willing to get up early enough to fetch fresh bread for breakfast, enough is bought in the evening for next morning's *petit déjeuner*; but this used to be considered the sign of a decadent household.

HORS-D'OEUVRE HOT AND COLD

BOUCHEES A LA MOUSSE DE POISSON
Miniature vol-au-vent with fish mousse filling

IMPERIAL/METRIC
1 lb./450 g. puff pastry
12 oz./350 g. fillet of
  whiting or codling
1 pint/6 dl. court
  bouillon with wine
  (see page 27)
½ pint/3 dl. thick béchamel
  sauce (see page 66)
2 eggs
1 tablespoon chopped
  parsley
1 tablespoon chopped
  chervil
salt and freshly ground
  white pepper
spinach, mushrooms or
  crab (see recipe)

AMERICAN
1 lb. puff paste
¾ lb. fillet of whiting
  or young cod
2½ cups court bouillon
  with wine (see page 27)
1¼ cups thick béchamel
  sauce (see page 66)
2 eggs
1 tablespoon chopped
  parsley
1 tablespoon chopped
  chervil
salt and freshly ground
  white pepper
spinach, mushrooms or
  crab (see recipe)

Roll out the pastry ¼ inch (½ cm.) thick. Cut 16 circles with a fluted biscuit cutter. Half cut through the tops of eight circles with a smaller cutter to show a definite impression. Place the eight other circles on a damp baking sheet, brush with water, lightly press the marked circles on top. Bake in a preheated hot oven (450°F., 230°C., Gas Mark 8) until golden brown, about 10–12 minutes. Remove the tops with the tip of a knife, press with the back of the blade twice to flatten. With the knife handle press in the centres of the bouchées. Meanwhile poach the fish for 10 minutes in the court bouillon. Strain 4 tablespoons of the cooking liquor into the sauce and beat in with the egg yolks. Drain the fish, flake and add to the sauce with the chopped herbs, seasoning to taste and one of the following:

1　4 oz. (100 g., 1 cup) button mushrooms, sliced and lightly sautéed in butter.

2　4 oz. (100 g., 1 cup) spinach, washed and cooked with a nut of butter, then sieved.

3　3 oz. (75 g., ½ cup) crab meat, plus 1 tablespoon cream. Beat the egg whites, fold into the mixture and use to fill the cases. Put on the lids, return to a moderate oven (350°F., 180°C., Gas Mark 4) for 10 minutes to heat through and serve hot.

Illustrated on page 20

BRIOCHES FOURRÉES
Stuffed brioches

IMPERIAL/METRIC	AMERICAN
4 small brioches	4 small brioches
	Filling
scrambled egg mixed with grated cheese	scrambled egg mixed with grated cheese

Remove the tops from the brioches and scoop out the centres to use for another dish (see pain de foie, page 18). Warm the brioches slightly in the oven, pile in the hot scrambled egg mixture and serve as a hot hors-d'oeuvre.

Note This is eaten with a knife and fork, which then rests on the *porte-couteau* ready for the entrée. If the first course requires a knife and fork, these are usually the ones intended for the main dish.

Variation

Blend 1 oz. (25 g., 2 tablespoons) pâté de foie with 1 tablespoon cream and fold in the stiffly beaten white of an egg. Put into the warmed brioches.

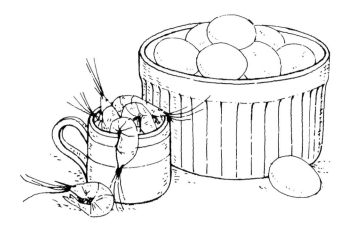

CROQUETTES DE CAMEMBERT
Camembert fritters

IMPERIAL/METRIC	AMERICAN
1 Camembert cheese, just ripe	1 Camembert cheese, just ripe
½ oz./15 g. butter	1 tablespoon butter
¾ oz./20 g. flour	3 tablespoons flour
5 tablespoons warm milk	6 tablespoons warm milk
1 tablespoon brandy or Calvados	1 tablespoon brandy or Calvados
¼ teaspoon freshly ground white pepper	¼ teaspoon freshly ground white pepper
1 egg	1 egg
1 tablespoon flour and 1 tablespoon toasted breadcrumbs for coating	1 tablespoon flour and 1 tablespoon dry bread crumbs for coating
oil for frying	oil for frying
	Garnish
parsley sprigs	parsley sprigs

Remove the rind from cheese, mash with a fork and beat until smooth. Make a roux with the butter and flour and add the milk and the brandy, beating vigorously to form a thick white sauce. Season with pepper and cool. Mix in the Camembert to make a firm croquette mixture. Roll with floured hands into walnut-sized cork-shaped croquettes. Beat the egg with 2 tablespoons cold water and use to coat the croquettes. Roll at once in a mixture of flour and breadcrumbs then deep-fry quickly in hot oil until golden brown. Drain on kitchen paper and serve garnished with parsley sprigs.

Note These are too rich for a supper dish but two or three per person make an excellent meal starter.

THON A LA MIROMESNIL
Tuna fish cream

IMPERIAL/METRIC	AMERICAN
8 oz./225 g. cooked fresh or canned tuna fish	½ lb. cooked fresh or canned tuna
3 tablespoons thick cream	¼ cup heavy cream
1 tablespoon mayonnaise	1 tablespoon mayonnaise
salt and pepper	salt and pepper
cayenne pepper	cayenne pepper
1 clove garlic, crushed	1 clove garlic, crushed
	To serve
black olives	ripe olives
hot toast fingers	hot toast fingers

Bone, skin and flake the fish. Pass through a sieve or blend to a cream in a liquidiser. Stir in the remaining ingredients and mix thoroughly. Serve chilled with black olives and fingers of hot toast.

OEUFS DURS AUX CREVETTES
Shrimp-stuffed eggs

IMPERIAL/METRIC	AMERICAN
4 eggs	4 eggs
6 oz./175 g. peeled shrimps	1 cup shelled shrimp
½ oz./15 g. butter	1 tablespoon butter
salt and freshly ground white pepper	salt and freshly ground white pepper
lettuce leaves	lettuce leaves
4 tablespoons mayonnaise (see page 67)	⅓ cup mayonnaise (see page 67)
	Garnish
cayenne pepper	cayenne pepper
chopped parsley	chopped parsley

Boil the eggs for 12 minutes, crack the shells and plunge the eggs into cold water for 30 minutes to prevent discolouration. Shell the eggs, slice in half lengthwise and carefully remove the yolks. Pound together the peeled shrimps and egg yolks, then blend in the butter and seasonings. Stuff the egg whites with the mixture and arrange them on a bed of lettuce. Spoon the mayonnaise over each half egg. Sprinkle with cayenne, top each egg with a little chopped parsley and serve cold.

OEUFS EN GELEE
Eggs in tarragon jelly

IMPERIAL/METRIC	AMERICAN
4 eggs	4 eggs
½ pint/3 dl. clear consommé	1¼ cups clear consommé
¼ oz./10 g. gelatine	2 teaspoons gelatin
1 tablespoon tarragon vinegar	1 tablespoon tarragon vinegar
2 tablespoons Madeira	3 tablespoons Madeira
2 oz./50 g. ham, chopped	¼ cup chopped ham
fresh tarragon leaves	fresh tarragon leaves

Boil the eggs. Plunge them into cold water to prevent discolouration. Heat 2 tablespoons of the consommé and sprinkle in the gelatine. Stir until dissolved then whisk into the remaining cold consommé with the vinegar and Madeira. Chill until cold but not set. Divide the ham among four cocotte dishes. Shell the eggs and put one in each dish. Top with a few tarragon leaves and spoon over the aspic before it begins to set. There should be just enough to cover the eggs.

Note This is definitely a summer dish calling for fresh tarragon only. Traditionally the French like the eggs to be soft-boiled (the yolks remaining soft while the whites are just set) but the majority of English people might prefer them cooked for about 8 minutes.

ESCARGOTS FARCIS
Stuffed snails

IMPERIAL/METRIC	AMERICAN
2 oz./50 g. butter	$\frac{1}{4}$ cup butter
2 cloves garlic, minced	2 cloves garlic, ground
1 shallot, minced	1 shallot, ground
1 tablespoon chopped parsley	1 tablespoon chopped parsley
1 tablespoon fine white breadcrumbs	1 tablespoon fine white bread crumbs
salt and freshly ground black pepper	salt and freshly ground black pepper
24 snails, cooked	24 snails, cooked

Pound together the butter, garlic, shallot, parsley, breadcrumbs and seasoning. Chill. If the snails are fresh, wash carefully, cover with cold water, bring to the boil and simmer for 45 minutes or until they can easily be detached from the shells. Remove, rinse the shells, replace the snails and seal in firmly with the stuffing. Arrange in dimpled snail platters or on a baking sheet (I sometimes put two each into patty tins so they stand up well), and put in a hot oven (425°F., 220°C., Gas Mark 7) for 8–10 minutes. As an hors-d'oeuvre, this quantity serves four.

Note Do not be tempted to experiment with garden snails. In France, snails are raised for the table and starved for a week before cooking to make them safe to eat. Canned snails have serving instructions on the can.

GRENOUILLES SAUTEES
Fried frogs' legs

IMPERIAL/METRIC	AMERICAN
8 oz./225 g. canned frogs' legs	$\frac{1}{2}$ lb. canned frogs' legs
juice of 1 lemon	juice of 1 lemon
salt and freshly ground black pepper	salt and freshly ground black pepper
milk and flour for coating	milk and flour for coating
4 oz./100 g. unsalted butter	$\frac{1}{2}$ cup sweet butter
1 tablespoon oil	1 tablespoon oil
1 clove garlic, crushed	1 clove garlic, crushed
2 tablespoons chopped parsley	3 tablespoons chopped parsley

Drain the legs well. Sprinkle with lemon juice, salt and pepper. Pass them through milk and then coat lightly in flour. Heat the butter and oil and fry the legs in them until just tender, 3–4 minutes. Drain on absorbent kitchen paper. Serve sprinkled with the crushed garlic and chopped parsley. At the last moment, pour over the butter from the pan.

Note Fresh frogs' legs, rarely available here, are at their best in the summer. Separate the thighs from the body with a sharp knife, remove and discard the feet, skin and skewer out flat. Soak in iced water for 2–3 hours and treat in the same way as the canned legs.

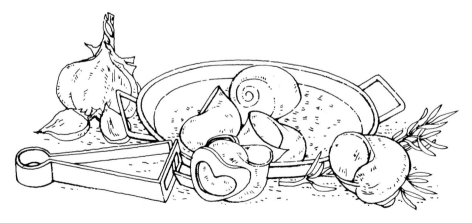

CHAMPIGNONS A LA GRECQUE
Greek style mushrooms

IMPERIAL/METRIC	AMERICAN
1 small onion	1 small onion
4 tablespoons olive oil	⅓ cup olive oil
1 lb./450 g. button mushrooms	4 cups button mushrooms
4 tablespoons white wine	⅓ cup white wine
1 tablespoon tomato purée	1 tablespoon tomato paste
juice of 1 lemon	juice of 1 lemon
1 bay leaf	1 bay leaf
½ teaspoon ground coriander	½ teaspoon ground coriander
salt and freshly ground white pepper	salt and freshly ground white pepper

Finely chop the onion. Heat the oil in a flameproof casserole and fry the onion in it until softened.
Add the mushrooms and toss until all are well coated.
Add the white wine, tomato purée mixed with the lemon juice, bay leaf and seasonings. Cover, lower the heat and simmer for 8 minutes, or until the mushrooms are just tender. Remove the bay leaf, strain off the mushrooms and reduce the liquid by about one third. Pour over the mushrooms. Allow to cool, in the liquid, and serve chilled.

POIREAUX A LA PROVENCALE
Leeks from Provence

IMPERIAL/METRIC	AMERICAN
6 oz./175 g. lean ham	⅓ lb. lean ham
2 lb./900 g. small leeks	2 lb. small leeks
2 tablespoons oil	3 tablespoons oil
8 oz./225 g. tomatoes	½ lb. tomatoes
juice of 1 lemon	juice of 1 lemon
salt and freshly ground black pepper	salt and freshly ground black pepper
12 black olives	12 ripe olives
1 sprig thyme	1 sprig thyme
Garnish	
chopped parsley	chopped parsley

Cut the ham into thin strips. Clean the leeks thoroughly and chop the white part only into 2-inch (5-cm.) lengths. Heat the oil in a large sauté pan and add the leeks and ham. Cover and cook gently for 10 minutes. Skin, deseed and chop the tomatoes. Add to the leeks, together with the lemon juice. Season well, stir in the black olives and thyme and cook uncovered for 10 minutes. Garnish with chopped parsley and serve chilled.

POIVRONS FARCIS
Stuffed green peppers

IMPERIAL/METRIC	AMERICAN
2 oz./50 g. butter	¼ cup butter
2 oz./50 g. long-grain rice	¼ cup long-grain rice
¼ pint/1½ dl. water	⅔ cup water
salt and pepper	salt and pepper
1 sprig thyme	1 sprig thyme
2 oz./50 g. lean ham, chopped	¼ cup chopped lean ham
4 green peppers	4 green sweet peppers
Sauce	
6 medium-sized tomatoes	6 medium-sized tomatoes
1 oz./25 g. butter	2 tablespoons butter
1 onion, chopped	1 onion, chopped
1 tablespoon lemon juice	1 tablespoon lemon juice
about ¼ pint /1½ dl. chicken stock	about ⅔ cup chicken bouillon

Melt the butter in a fairly deep saucepan. Stir in the rice. Add the water, salt, pepper and thyme. Bring to the boil, cover and simmer gently for 10 minutes. Remove the sprig of thyme, drain the rice and mix with the chopped ham. Slice off the stem end of the peppers and carefully remove the seeds. Fill the peppers with the rice and ham stuffing and replace the lids. Stand upright in an ovenproof casserole. To make the sauce, peel, halve and deseed the tomatoes. Heat the butter in a sauté pan and add the chopped onion. Fry until lightly browned then add the tomatoes, salt and pepper and lemon juice. Just cover with chicken stock and bring to the boil. Cover and simmer for 10 minutes. Sieve or liquidise the sauce and pour over the green peppers. Cover and cook in a cool oven (300°F., 150°C., Gas Mark 2) for 1 hour. Serve hot or cold.

LES CRUDITES
Vegetable platter

This type of hors-d'oeuvre, composed entirely of raw vegetables with delicate dressings, or with none, becomes more and more popular. It is slimming, and healthy. The cheaper restaurants in Paris are crammed at mid-day with secretaries who cannot take the long journey home by Métro to eat with *Maman*, making a meal of *'crudités'*. One could do worse. Here is a typical selection:

Cucumber Peeled, sliced, salted until limp, then rinsed and served soft rather than crisp, perhaps sprinkled with finely chopped parsley.

Cauliflower Broken into tiny florets, sometimes blanched for 1 minute then sprinkled with a little vinaigrette dressing.

Carrots Very young ones, peeled or scraped and cut into thin fingers.

Radishes Cleaned and left with a respectable 'tuft' of stem to grasp while eating, or cut into roses or concertinas. A milder radish is preferred in France. Very hot ones are offered with cries of *'Prenez garde!'*

Celery Nicely trimmed stalks are halved lengthwise and cut in bite-sized pieces.

Tomatoes Blanched and peeled, sometimes seeded, and sprinkled with finely chopped shallots or chives mingled with parsley.

As a tempting centrepiece, serve potato salad in mayonnaise, or *celeri-rémoulade*. Celeriac, neglected here but much loved in France, has a bulbous root which is cut into matchsticks and tossed in mustard-flavoured mayonnaise.

Butter is not served with bread, as such, at the French table except for breakfast. In a mixed platter of hors-d'oeuvre, a fancy pat of butter may be part of the pattern ranged round the rim, as a few people like buttered bread with their first course. I have often watched, with secret pleasure, an American or British tourist solemnly consuming it in one single mouthful wondering why that particular item tasted so exactly like what it was – a pat of unsalted butter.

HORS-D'OEUVRE VARIES
Mixed hors-d'oeuvre

Contrast is the thing. Radishes with butter (to help down the fresh baking of lunchtime bread) is the simplest basis, but in most homes three varieties will be offered:

Raw crisp vegetables Radishes, or any *crudité*.

Cooked vegetables in vinaigrette Green beans, flageolets, haricots blancs, artichoke hearts. This item usually represents the carefully hoarded leftovers of the green or other vegetables from the previous day's dinner.

Something in mayonnaise Hard-boiled eggs, mushrooms, a tempting mixture of cooked white fish, well flaked, with shellfish such as a few shrimps, or prawns.

Something meaty Wafer-thin slices of ham, salami, or pork brawn from the *charcuterie*. If not, something fishy, such as anchovies or sardines in oil, or at the very least some black or green olives.

It is surprising how good carefully prepared vegetables are cold, even without vinaigrette. Not boiled cabbage, but lightly cooked and nutty-tasting leeks, aubergines, sweet peppers, artichokes, or a *mélange* of several, as in ratatouille.

PATES AND TERRINES

TERRINE DE LIEVRE A L'ANCIENNE
Terrine of hare

IMPERIAL/METRIC	AMERICAN
1 hare	1 hare
2 tablespoons brandy	3 tablespoons brandy
4 black peppercorns	4 black peppercorns
8 oz./225 g. very fat bacon	$\frac{1}{2}$ lb. very fat bacon
8 oz./225 g. pork sausage meat	$\frac{1}{2}$ lb. pork sausage meat
$\frac{1}{2}$ teaspoon salt	$\frac{1}{2}$ teaspoon salt
$\frac{1}{4}$ teaspoon freshly ground black pepper	$\frac{1}{4}$ teaspoon freshly ground black pepper
$\frac{1}{2}$ teaspoon ground coriander	$\frac{1}{2}$ teaspoon ground coriander
2 eggs	2 eggs
$\frac{1}{4}$ pint/1$\frac{1}{2}$ dl. red wine	$\frac{2}{3}$ cup red wine
2 carrots, chopped	2 carrots, chopped
1 onion, chopped	1 onion, chopped
bacon fat for barding	bacon fat or salt pork for barding

Illustrated on page 17

Carefully skin the hare. Joint it and remove the flesh from the bones, keeping the meat from both sides of the saddle whole. Marinate the fillet meat, cut lengthwise into strips, in the brandy, seasoned with 4 peppercorns, for 4–6 hours. Remove and discard the peppercorns. Mince or finely chop the fat bacon and remaining meat of the hare, mix with the sausage meat, season with salt, pepper and coriander and bind with the lightly beaten eggs. Heat the wine with the chopped carrot and onion, adding the bones from the hare, and cook for 5 minutes, to make a concentrated meat stock (*fumet*). Strain and add to the mixture. Line a terrine mould with wide strips of bacon fat and fill with alternate layers of the mixture and the fillet strips, rounding the top and barding with a lattice work of bacon fat strips. Cover and cook in a moderate oven (350°F., 180°C., Gas Mark 4) for 2 hours. Cool; and allow to mature for several days before serving.

Note This recipe is prepared with sighs by my Tante Joséphine, who finds it worth while when it is consumed with delight by that great hunter of game, Oncle Emile, who often bags a hare in autumn if he remembers to take out his long-distance glasses as well as his shotgun.

PATE DE CAMPAGNE
Country pâté

IMPERIAL/METRIC	AMERICAN
8 rashers streaky bacon	8 slices bacon
4 oz./100 g. pig's liver, minced	$\frac{1}{2}$ cup ground pork liver
8 oz./225 g. lean pork, minced	$1\frac{1}{4}$ cups lean ground pork
8 oz./225 g. veal, diced	1 cup lean ground veal
4 oz./100 g. belly pork, minced	$\frac{1}{4}$ cup ground fat back
2 cloves garlic, crushed	2 cloves garlic, crushed
3 tablespoons brandy or Calvados	$\frac{1}{4}$ cup brandy or Calvados (applejack)
$\frac{1}{4}$ teaspoon ground mace	$\frac{1}{4}$ teaspoon ground mace
$\frac{1}{4}$ teaspoon ground bay leaves	$\frac{1}{4}$ teaspoon ground bay leaves
$\frac{1}{4}$ teaspoon dried basil	$\frac{1}{4}$ teaspoon dried basil
$\frac{1}{2}$ teaspoon salt	$\frac{1}{2}$ teaspoon salt
$\frac{1}{4}$ teaspoon freshly ground black pepper	$\frac{1}{4}$ teaspoon freshly ground black pepper

Derind the bacon rashers and stretch with the back of a knife blade. Use to line a 2-lb. (1-kg.) loaf tin or oval terrine. Mix together thoroughly all the other ingredients and press into the prepared tin, folding over the ends of the bacon rashers. Cover with foil and stand the tin in a bain-marie with 1 inch ($2\frac{1}{2}$ cm.) of water. Cook in a cool oven (300°F., 150°C., Gas Mark 2) for 2 hours, until the pâté shrinks slightly from the sides of the tin. Remove from the water and cool. Store, covered, in the refrigerator for at least 2 days to mature. Release the edges with a knife and turn out. Serve with fresh bread.

MOUSSE DE FOIE DE VOLAILLE
Chicken liver mousse

IMPERIAL/METRIC	AMERICAN
12 oz./350 g. chicken livers	$\frac{3}{4}$ lb. chicken livers
$\frac{1}{4}$ teaspoon grated nutmeg	$\frac{1}{4}$ teaspoon grated nutmeg
salt and freshly ground white pepper	salt and freshly ground white pepper
4 tablespoons Madeira	$\frac{1}{3}$ cup Madeira
1 tablespoon brandy	1 tablespoon brandy
1 oz./25 g. butter	2 tablespoons butter
1 tablespoon chopped onion	1 tablespoon chopped onion
1 clove garlic, crushed	1 clove garlic, crushed
1 egg, separated	1 egg, separated
4 tablespoons cream	$\frac{1}{3}$ cup cream

Marinade the chicken livers overnight with the seasonings in the Madeira and brandy. Drain, reserving the marinade. Melt the butter and fry the onion and garlic gently until soft, then add the chicken livers and cook for a few minutes until firm but still pink inside. Boil the marinade in the same pan until reduced by half, add to the livers. Beat the egg yolk into the cream until it begins to thicken. Sieve or liquidise the livers, then blend in the cream, or beat it in. Lastly, fold in the stiffly beaten egg white. Pack into individual cocottes, chill, and serve with melba toast.

Note This is the traditional first course served at a great gathering when almost every leaf on the family tree is present – the *dîner de reveillon*, or Christmas dinner, French style, which takes place very late on Christmas Eve, after those pious enough to go have attended Midnight Mass.

Terrine de lièvre à l'ancienne (page 15)

PAIN DE FOIE
Liver pâté loaf

IMPERIAL/METRIC	AMERICAN
4 oz./100 g. fat green bacon	¼ lb. unsmoked bacon
4 oz./100 g. brioche (see note)	¼ lb. brioche (see note)
4 fl. oz./1 dl. warm milk	½ cup warm milk
8 oz./225 g. chicken, duck or turkey livers, chopped	1 cup chopped chicken, duck or turkey livers
good pinch freshly ground pepper	good pinch freshly ground pepper
1 clove garlic, crushed	1 clove garlic, crushed
4 eggs, separated	4 eggs, separated
4 bay leaves	4 bay leaves

Derind the bacon and dice. Soak the brioche in the milk for a few minutes, squeeze lightly. Mix together the soaked brioche, chopped raw liver, diced bacon, pepper and garlic and mince together finely. Fold in the lightly beaten egg yolks, or liquidise all these ingredients together. Beat the egg whites lightly and fold into the mixture. Grease a terrine mould and turn in the mixture, arranging the bay leaves on top. Cover with a lid or foil and cook in a moderate oven (350°F., 180°C., Gas Mark 4) for 1 hour, removing the cover for the last 5 minutes. Serve from the terrine.

Note Use the centres of the brioches, see brioches fourrées, page 10.

PATE DE TRUITE FUMEE
Smoked trout pâté

IMPERIAL/METRIC	AMERICAN
2 large smoked trout	2 large smoked trout
4 oz./100 g. demi-sel cheese	½ cup demi-sel or other soft cream cheese
2 tablespoons cream	3 tablespoons cream
8 oz./225 g. butter, softened	1 cup softened butter
2 tablespoons lemon juice	3 tablespoons lemon juice
salt and freshly ground black pepper	salt and freshly ground black pepper
Garnish	
1 gherkin	1 dill pickled cucumber

Skin and bone the fish and pound with pestle and mortar, gradually working in the cheese, cream and butter, or blend all together in a liquidiser. Finish with the lemon juice and seasoning to taste. Turn into ramekins and chill. Garnish with a gherkin fan and serve with melba toast.

BRANDADE
Salt cod pâté

IMPERIAL/METRIC	AMERICAN
8 oz./225 g. salt cod	½ lb. salt cod
2 cloves garlic, crushed	2 cloves garlic, crushed
4 fl. oz./1 dl. olive oil	½ cup olive oil
4 tablespoons cream	⅓ cup cream
1 tablespoon lemon juice	1 tablespoon lemon juice
salt and freshly ground black pepper	salt and freshly ground black pepper

If possible soak the fish for a few hours in water or milk. Cut the fish into small pieces and poach for about 10 minutes in plenty of water, until just tender. Drain, bone and skin. Pound the fish and garlic together with a pestle and mortar, adding the oil drop by drop, or liquidise in a blender. Turn into a heavy pan and cook very gently, stirring constantly, for 5 minutes, adding the cream a little at a time. Remove from heat, stir in the lemon juice and seasoning to taste (the amount of salt depending on how heavily the fish is salted). Serve as other pâtés with hot toast.

Note Smoked haddock can be used instead of salt cod. Americans have taught my French cousins (who consider it a highly prized foreign delicacy) to call it finnan haddie, pronounced 'Finand a dit'. . . . 'Mais qu'est-ce qu'il a dit, ce M. Finand?' the children always ask, highly intrigued by the fish with the odd-sounding name.

SOUPS

SOUPE A L'OIGNON
Onion soup

IMPERIAL/METRIC	AMERICAN
2 oz./50 g. butter	¼ cup butter
1 lb./450 g. large onions, sliced	1 lb. large onions, sliced
salt and freshly ground black pepper	salt and freshly ground black pepper
1 teaspoon flour	1 teaspoon flour
1½ pints/scant litre beef stock	4 cups beef bouillon
8 thick slices French bread	8 thick slices French bread
2 oz./50 g. Gruyère cheese, grated	½ cup grated Gruyère cheese
½ oz./15 g. Parmesan cheese, grated	2 tablespoons grated Parmesan cheese

Melt the butter, add the onion rings and seasoning and fry gently until the onions are browned, about 20 minutes. Stir in the flour, add the stock, cover and simmer for 10 minutes. Adjust seasoning. Toast the bread lightly on both sides and place in the bottom of a warmed soup tureen, or two slices in each soup bowl. Mix together the cheeses and sprinkle over the bread. Pour in the hot soup gently so that the bread slices float. Place under a hot grill until the cheese begins to bubble and turn brown. (Choose dishes that will stand heat.)

Note Breaking up the bread and the stringy melting cheese with your soup spoon is quite a job to accomplish elegantly, but well worth the effort. This soup seems a little watery to our taste but a true French *soupe* should be hardly thickened.

POTAGE BONNE FEMME
Vegetable soup

The classic style of vegetable soup in which a variety of chopped vegetables is first fried gently in butter, then cooked in stock until tender, often makes an economical evening meal. Sometimes shredded cabbage is added or a handful of finely chopped sorrel (or spinach with a little lemon juice) and the soup is served with a generous dollop of butter melting in the centre of the tureen. My cousin Micheline, who is an elegant Parisienne, often serves it, and says it should be called *potage de femme d'affaires*, as it is a business woman's standby when the *circulation* makes her late in coming home.

Bouchées à la mousse de poisson (page 9)

Potage de pois cassés au lard (page 23)

SOUPE AU PISTOU
Garlic vegetable soup

IMPERIAL/METRIC	AMERICAN
4 oz./100 g. dried haricot beans	½ cup navy beans
1 tablespoon olive oil	1 tablespoon olive oil
1 onion, chopped	1 onion, chopped
salt and pepper	salt and pepper
2 pints/generous litre water	5 cups water
8 oz./225 g. French beans, sliced	½ lb. green beans, sliced
3 small courgettes, chopped	2 zucchini, chopped
1 carrot, chopped	1 carrot, chopped
1 leek, sliced	1 leek, sliced
2 potatoes, diced	2 potatoes, diced

Pistou sauce

IMPERIAL/METRIC	AMERICAN
3 cloves garlic	3 cloves garlic
6 sprigs basil	6 sprigs basil
3 tablespoons olive oil	¼ cup olive oil

Soak the haricot beans overnight. Heat the oil in a large saucepan and use to fry the onion until soft and just turning golden. Season and add the water. Bring to the boil. Add the drained haricot beans, French beans, courgettes, carrot, leek and potatoes. Cook quickly for 10 minutes, or until vegetables are soft. To make the pistou sauce, mash the garlic cloves and pound together with the basil. Gradually add the oil, drop by drop, as for mayonnaise. Mix thoroughly then stir into the soup. Continue cooking gently for 5 minutes. Serve at once and hand bowls of grated Parmesan separately.

Note This recipe comes from Martigues, near Marseille. It is called 'lizard soup' by my nieces, because when we have it on the terrace in the evenings, the lizards seem to smell it and all gather round to watch as though they wanted to taste it. It does smell rather strong, but is quite delicious.

COTRIADE BRETONNE
Breton fish soup

IMPERIAL/METRIC	AMERICAN
2 oz./50 g. butter	¼ cup butter
1 onion, sliced	1 onion, sliced
3 pints/1¾ litres hot water	2 quarts hot water
salt and pepper	salt and pepper
1 clove garlic, crushed	1 clove garlic, crushed
pinch ground cloves	pinch ground cloves
3 carrots, chopped	3 carrots, chopped
1 large potato, sliced	1 large potato, sliced
bouquet garni	bouquet garni
2½ lb./generous kg. mixed fish	2½ lb. mixed fish
1 tablespoon tomato purée	1 tablespoon tomato paste
wine vinegar	wine vinegar
pepper	pepper
sliced French bread, toasted	sliced French bread, toasted

Melt ½ oz. (15 g., 1 tablespoon) of the butter in a large saucepan and fry the onion until golden brown. Add the water, salt, pepper, garlic and ground cloves. Bring to the boil and add the carrots, potatoes and bouquet garni. Cook for 30 minutes. Add the fish, bring to the boil and continue cooking for a further 15 minutes. Drain the fish and keep hot. Stir the tomato purée into the liquor and simmer for 10 minutes. Butter the toast. Strain the soup, remove the bouquet garni, and place the vegetables on another hot serving dish. Sprinkle them and the fish with wine vinegar and plenty of pepper. Serve the soup poured over the toast and place the vegetables and the fish in the centre of the table for guests to help themselves.

BISQUE DE CRABE
Crab soup

IMPERIAL/METRIC	AMERICAN
2 small crabs	2 small crabs
1½ pints/scant litre court bouillon with wine (see page 27)	4 cups court bouillon with wine (see page 27)
2 oz./50 g. long-grain rice	¼ cup long-grain rice
2 teaspoons tomato purée	2 teaspoons tomato paste
2 egg yolks	2 egg yolks

Cook the crabs in the court bouillon, drain, cool and remove all edible meat from the shells. Strain the liquid and cook the rice in it with the tomato purée. Strain off the rice and pound with the crab meat with a pestle and mortar, or liquidise in a blender with a few tablespoons of the strained liquor. Return to the saucepan of hot liquor and reheat to boiling point. Place the egg yolks in the bottom of a warmed soup tureen and gradually beat in a little of the hot soup. Then add the remaining soup all at once and continue beating until smooth. Serve croûtons separately.

Note A more sophisticated bisque can be made with lobster and the addition of a little cream and brandy. In France, you could certainly buy the shellfish live in the market, but if you find you cannot obtain them, use canned crab meat, with its juices, and make the court bouillon with fish trimmings.

POTAGE DE POIS CASSES AU LARD
Pea soup with bacon

IMPERIAL/METRIC	AMERICAN
1 lb./450 g. split peas	2 cups split peas
1 teaspoon salt	1 teaspoon salt
2 leeks	2 leeks
1 oz./25 g. butter	2 tablespoons butter
½ pint/3 dl. stock	1¼ cups bouillon
2 slices fat bacon	2 slices bacon or salt pork
2 tablespoons chopped parsley	3 tablespoons chopped parsley
Illustrated on page 21	

Soak the peas overnight in 2 pints (a generous litre, 5 cups) water. Put into a pan with the soaking water, salt and the green part only of the leeks, finely chopped, and cook until the peas are soft, about 2 hours. Sieve or liquidise, stir in the butter and add sufficient stock to make a thick creamy consistency. Cut the bacon slices into thin strips and render out the fat until brown and crisp, to make *lardons*. Serve the soup scattered with lardons and chopped parsley.

Note The fat from the *lardons* is usually added to the soup as well as the butter unless the diet forbids, or used to fry croûtons to sprinkle on top.

POTAGE ST. GERMAIN
Garden pea soup

IMPERIAL/METRIC	AMERICAN
6 spring onions	6 scallions
2 oz./50 g. butter	¼ cup butter
1 lb./450 g. fresh garden peas	1 lb. fresh garden peas
6 lettuce leaves	6 lettuce leaves
salt and pepper	salt and pepper
½ teaspoon sugar	½ teaspoon sugar
1¼ pints/¾ litre chicken stock	3 cups chicken bouillon
Garnish	
croûtons	croûtons
cream	cream

Clean and chop the spring onions, including most of the green top. Melt the butter in a heavy saucepan and stir in the prepared vegetables, salt and sugar. Cover and cook gently for 5 minutes. Add the stock and continue simmering for approximately 10 minutes. The peas should then be quite tender. Sieve or liquidise, check the seasoning and reheat. Serve garnished with croûtons and a swirl of thick cream.

Cabillaud à la ratatouille (page 30)

Omelette à l'oseille (page 35)

CREME DE CRESSON
Watercress soup

IMPERIAL/METRIC	AMERICAN
3 tablespoons chopped onion	¼ cup chopped onion
2 oz./50 g. butter	¼ cup butter
1 medium-sized potato, sliced	1 medium-sized potato, sliced
salt and freshly ground black pepper	salt and freshly ground black pepper
2 bunches watercress	2 bunches watercress
¾ pint/4 dl. milk	2 cups milk
½ pint/3 dl. chicken stock	1¼ cups chicken bouillon
2 egg yolks	2 egg yolks
2 tablespoons cream	3 tablespoons cream

Sauté the chopped onion in the butter until transparent, then add the sliced potato, seasoning and just sufficient water to cover. Simmer until the vegetables become mushy, about 10 minutes. Meanwhile wash the watercress, reserving some tiny sprigs for the garnish. Chop the remainder finely and add to the pan with the milk and stock. Bring to the boil, lower the heat, cover and simmer for 15 minutes. Sieve or liquidise the soup and return to the pan all but a few tablespoons. Beat the egg yolks and cream into this, then gradually stir into the soup as it reheats. Do not allow it to boil. Serve garnished with watercress sprigs.

Note This soup reheats very well, provided it is not boiled, and seems to develop more flavour the next day. Babies love it, perhaps because of the pretty green colour, and they always get a big bowlful. Probably that is why my family recipe has no garlic.

CHIFFONADE
Lettuce soup

IMPERIAL/METRIC	AMERICAN
2 young lettuces	2 young lettuces
1 oz./25 g. butter	2 tablespoons butter
1 oz./25 g. rice	2 tablespoons rice
1½ pints/scant litre boiling chicken stock	4 cups boiling chicken bouillon
salt and pepper	salt and pepper
	Garnish
lemon curls	lemon curls

Wash the lettuce, discard the outside leaves and shred the remainder finely. Melt the butter in a heavy saucepan. Add the lettuce and cook gently for 5 minutes, turning regularly. Add the rice and stock. Season well and cook for 10 minutes. Serve very hot, garnished with lemon curls made by paring thin strips of zest with a canelle knife.

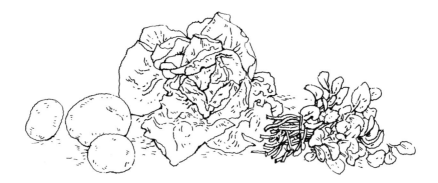

FISH AND SHELLFISH

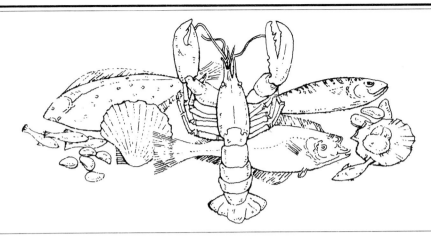

COURT BOUILLON

With vinegar Put in a large pan a thinly sliced onion and carrot, bouquet garni, 1 teaspoon salt, 4 white peppercorns, 1 pint (6 dl., 2½ cups) water and ¼ pint (1½ dl., ⅔ cup) wine vinegar. Simmer, covered, for 20–30 minutes. Strain and use to poach fish and shellfish.

With wine Substitute ½ pint (3 dl., 1¼ cups) wine for the vinegar. Part wine and part vinegar can be used, especially for strongly flavoured or oily fish such as mackerel.

Fish fumet Add the head, bones and trimmings from the fish to the court bouillon.

FILLETS DE SOLE CENDRILLON
Sole with artichokes

IMPERIAL/METRIC	AMERICAN
2 large sole, filleted	2 large sole, filleted
salt and freshly ground white pepper	salt and freshly ground white pepper
2 tablespoons lemon juice	3 tablespoons lemon juice
2 oz./50 g. butter	¼ cup butter
½ oz./15 g. flour	1 tablespoon flour
½ pint/3 dl. fish fumet (see above)	1¼ cups fish fumet (see above)
4 tablespoons cream	⅓ cup cream
2 egg yolks	2 egg yolks
1 7¾-oz./219-g. can artichoke bottoms	1 7¾-oz. can artichoke bottoms
Garnish	
4 pats parsley butter	4 pats parsley butter

Ask the fishmonger to skin and fillet the fish and give you the heads, bones and trimmings to make the fumet.

Butter a shallow ovenproof dish and lay the sole fillets neatly in it. Season with salt and pepper, sprinkle with the lemon juice and an equal amount of water, dot with a little of the butter. Cover and poach in a moderate oven (350°F., 180°C., Gas Mark 4) for 15–20 minutes. In a small saucepan, make a roux with the remaining butter and the flour. Stir in the liquid drained from the fish, and sufficient of the fumet to make a thin pouring sauce. Stir in the cream and beat in the egg yolks. Remove from the heat. Warm the artichoke bottoms in the liquid from the can. Drain, reserving four for the garnish, and sieve or liquidise the remainder, with a few tablespoons of the fumet. Put the artichoke purée in a warm shallow serving dish, arrange the sole fillets neatly on top and garnish with the remaining artichoke bottoms, each containing a pat of parsley butter.

Pain d'aubergines (page 39)

Tourte à la viande (page 40)

SARDINES FRITES A LA SAUCE VERTE
Fried sardines with green sauce

IMPERIAL/METRIC	AMERICAN
12 fresh sardines or 1½ lb./675 g. sprats	12 fresh sardines or 1½ lb. sprats
salt and freshly ground black pepper	salt and freshly ground black pepper
small bottle light ale	small bottle light beer
4–6 oz./150–175 g. seasoned flour	1–1½ cups seasoned flour
oil for deep-frying	oil for deep-frying

Sauce verte

IMPERIAL/METRIC	AMERICAN
8 oz./225 g. sorrel or spinach	½ lb. sorrel or spinach
knob of butter	knob of butter
1 teaspoon Dijon mustard	1 teaspoon Dijon mustard
pinch powdered saffron	pinch powdered saffron
4 tablespoons lemon juice	⅓ cup lemon juice
1 tablespoon chopped parsley	1 tablespoon chopped parsley
1 tablespoon chopped chervil	1 tablespoon chopped chervil
½ pint/3 dl. mayonnaise (see page 67)	1¼ cups mayonnaise (see page 67)

Clean the fish, sprinkle with salt and pepper, pass through the light ale and coat in seasoned flour. Deep-fry in very hot oil in a basket until golden brown. Drain and serve hot and crisp. To make the sauce, wash the sorrel and cook until just limp with a tiny knob of butter. Put through a sieve or liquidise. Beat the mustard, saffron, lemon juice, sieved sorrel and fresh herbs with the mayonnaise. Serve separately, with *pommes vapeur* (steamed new potatoes).

Illustrated on page 32

Note In the Midi, sauce verte is sometimes considered too sophisticated when there is a fresh catch of sardines available for frying. The sauce on such occasions is simply made by beating soft goat's cheese, such as Saint Marcellin, with lots and lots of crushed garlic.

CABILLAUD A LA RATATOUILLE
Cod steaks with ratatouille

IMPERIAL/METRIC	AMERICAN
4 thin cod steaks	4 thin cod steaks
2 tablespoons seasoned flour	3 tablespoons seasoned flour
1 tablespoon curry powder	1 tablespoon curry powder
oil for frying	oil for frying

Ratatouille

IMPERIAL/METRIC	AMERICAN
4 tomatoes, skinned and sliced	4 tomatoes, skinned and sliced
2 cloves garlic, crushed	2 cloves garlic, crushed
2 onions, sliced	2 onions, sliced
1 small hot red pepper	1 small red chili pepper
3 courgettes, sliced	3 zucchini, sliced
1 small aubergine, sliced	1 small eggplant, sliced
½ teaspoon dried thyme	½ teaspoon dried thyme
1 bay leaf	1 bay leaf
1 sweet red pepper	1 sweet red pepper

First make the ratatouille. Cook the tomatoes, garlic, onions and hot pepper, covered, very gently until soft, about 5 minutes. Then add the courgettes, aubergine and herbs. Lastly, add the finely sliced and skinned sweet red pepper. (Skin by holding on a fork over an open flame, or putting in a hot oven for a few minutes.) Cook for a further 10 minutes and serve hot with the fried fish.

To cook the cod steaks, wash and dry them. Turn in the seasoned flour mixed with curry powder. Shallow-fry on both sides until golden brown in the oil, spooning it up over the sides to colour them evenly.

Illustrated on page 24

Note If preferred, poach the sliced sweet pepper without skinning in boiling water for 3 minutes before adding to the ratatouille. I always remove the hot red pepper before serving.

RAIE AU BEURRE NOIR
Skate with black butter

IMPERIAL/METRIC	AMERICAN
2 lb./900 g. wing of skate	2 lb. wing of skate
1 pint/6 dl. court bouillon with vinegar (see page 27)	5 cups court bouillon with vinegar (see page 27)
Black butter	
2 oz./50 g. butter	¼ cup butter
1 tablespoon vinegar	1 tablespoon vinegar
1 tablespoon capers	1 tablespoon capers

Wash and trim the skate and cut into four pieces. Lay the fish in the court bouillon and poach gently for 15 minutes. Drain well and lift off the skin on both sides. Arrange the fish on a warm serving dish and keep hot. Melt the butter in a small frying pan until it turns nut brown then pour it over the fish. Add the vinegar to the pan with the capers and reduce slightly. Pour over the fish and serve at once.

TRUITES AU BLEU
Poached trout

IMPERIAL/METRIC	AMERICAN
¼ pint/1½ dl. red wine	⅔ cup red wine
¼ pint/1½ dl. wine vinegar	⅔ cup wine vinegar
1 bay leaf	1 bay leaf
4 peppercorns	4 peppercorns
½ teaspoon salt	½ teaspoon salt
4 trout	4 trout
4 oz./100 g. butter, melted	½ cup melted butter
2 tablespoons capers	3 tablespoons capers

Place the wine, vinegar, bay leaf and seasoning in a saucepan and simmer for 20 minutes. Allow to stand for at least 1 hour. Simmer the fish in the liquor for 7–8 minutes, according to their size. Serve well drained with melted butter and capers poured over them.

Note The trout must be very fresh and in restaurants they will probably be killed by plunging into boiling vinegar, after you have chosen your live fish from the tank.

QUENELLES DE POISSON
Fish dumplings

IMPERIAL/METRIC	AMERICAN
3 large whiting or 2 codling	3 large whiting or 2 small cod
6 oz./175 g. butter	¾ cup butter
6 oz./175 g. white breadcrumbs	3 cups white bread crumbs
¼ pint/1½ dl. milk	⅔ cup milk
4 eggs	4 eggs
salt and freshly ground white pepper	salt and freshly ground white pepper

Skin and bone the fish and pound the flesh until smooth. Add the softened butter and the breadcrumbs soaked in the milk. Beat the mixture until it becomes a smooth firm paste, then beat in the eggs one by one. Season generously and allow to stand for at least 30 minutes. Roll into small cork shapes with floured hands. Poach in a large pan of lightly salted simmering water for 10 minutes. Do not let the water boil or the delicate flavour will be lost. Serve with a sauce made from fresh tomatoes.

Sardines frites à la sauce verte (page 30)

MAQUEREAUX AU VIN BLANC
Mackerel in white wine

IMPERIAL/METRIC	AMERICAN
4 mackerel	4 mackerel
½ pint/3 dl. dry white wine	1¼ cups dry white wine
¼ pint/1½ dl. wine vinegar	⅔ cup wine vinegar
1 large onion, chopped	1 large onion, chopped
1 medium-sized carrot, chopped	1 medium-sized carrot, chopped
4 lemon slices	4 lemon slices
1 clove garlic, crushed	1 clove garlic, crushed
8 peppercorns	8 peppercorns
bouquet garni	bouquet garni
salt	salt
Garnish	
sprigs of fennel	sprigs of fennel

Have the mackerel filleted. Put the fish bones, wine, vinegar, onion, carrot, lemon slices, garlic and seasonings in a pan and bring to the boil. Cover and simmer for 25 minutes. Strain the resulting stock over the mackerel fillets in a shallow pan. Poach the fish for 3 minutes only. Cool in the stock then remove. Reduce the liquid slightly, then spoon a little over the fish. Garnish with sprigs of fennel and serve chilled.

MOULES A LA MARINIERE
Mussels in white wine

This famous dish has many versions but a very simple one is favoured by my family. They can eat a litre of mussels each, prepared like this. In a huge pan, put 1 litre (1¾ pints, 1 quart) mussels, washed, weed removed, and firmly shut, for each person. Add a large sliced carrot and onion, plenty of thyme and chopped parsley, a few bay leaves and as many crushed garlic cloves as consideration for one's nearest and dearest will allow. Add ¼ pint (1½ dl., ⅔ cup) white wine per litre of mussels and salt and pepper to taste, bring to the boil and simmer, shaking the pan occasionally, until all the shells have opened. Dole out into soup bowls and provide plenty of bread so that none of the delicious juices are wasted.

COQUILLES DE FRUITS DE MER
Fish in the shell

IMPERIAL/METRIC	AMERICAN
6 scallops	6 scallops
1 pint/6 dl. mussels	2½ cups mussels
2 oz./50 g. butter	¼ cup butter
1 tablespoon grated onion	1 tablespoon grated onion
1 clove garlic, crushed	1 clove garlic, crushed
2 oz./50 g. mushrooms, sliced	½ cup sliced mushrooms
2 oz./50 g. white breadcrumbs	1 cup white bread crumbs
¼ pint/1½ dl. white wine	⅔ cup white wine
1 tablespoon lemon juice	1 tablespoon lemon juice
1 tablespoon chopped parsley	1 tablespoon chopped parsley
salt and freshly ground pepper	salt and freshly ground pepper

If the scallops and mussels are in the shell, put in a large pan in a moderate oven until they open. Remove from the shells and chop the white part and coral of the scallops with the bearded mussels. Melt half the butter and use to sauté lightly the onion, garlic and mushrooms. Mix with the chopped shellfish. Butter four deep scallop shells, sprinkle in half the breadcrumbs and fill the shells with the mushroom and fish mixture. Boil together the liquid from the shells (if available), or 4 tablespoons water, with the wine and lemon juice until reduced to about ¼ pint, and spoon over the shells. Combine the remaining breadcrumbs with the parsley and seasoning and spread over the shells. Melt the remaining butter and pour over. Bake uncovered in a moderate oven (350°F., 180°C., Gas Mark 4) for 15 minutes.

Note In Brittany the mixture is kept sufficiently dry to be eaten conveniently with a small fork. In Normandy the fish mixture is blended with béchamel sauce and cream, and sprinkled with cheese instead of breadcrumbs, then browned under the grill. This is better eaten with a spoon, or if with a fork, with plenty of bread to sop up the sauce.

EGG AND CHEESE DISHES

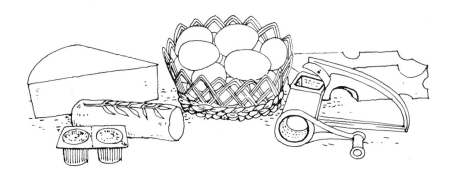

CREPES AUX CREVETTES
Shrimp pancakes

IMPERIAL/METRIC	AMERICAN
Basic crêpe batter	
2 eggs	2 eggs
½ pint milk	1¼ cups milk
4 oz./100 g. flour	1 cup flour
pinch salt	pinch salt
butter for frying	butter for frying
Filling	
2 oz./50 g. cooked peeled shrimps	⅓ cup cooked shelled shrimp
good pinch nutmeg	good pinch nutmeg
1 oz./25 g. butter	2 tablespoons butter
salt and freshly ground white pepper	salt and freshly ground white pepper
1 tablespoon cream	1 tablespoon cream

Make up the crêpe batter and leave to stand while you make the filling. Pound the shrimps, nutmeg, butter, salt and pepper to a paste. Dilute with the cream to a spreading consistency and warm gently. Cook the crêpes, spread each one with the warm shrimp mixture, roll up and place in an ovenproof dish and keep hot. Serve as soon as the last one is ready because the delicate flavour is impaired by keeping them for any length of time in the oven.

Note For parties, fold half the crêpes spread with shrimp butter in half then in four. Give each person a crêpe folded in four then another on top as follows: fold in half then bring the folds in to a central point and fold back on themselves, filling the centres with more shrimps and a slice of lemon.

CREPES AUX EPINARDS
Spinach pancakes

IMPERIAL/METRIC	AMERICAN
1 lb./450 g. spinach	1 lb. spinach
1 oz./25 g. butter	2 tablespoons butter
¼ teaspoon nutmeg	¼ teaspoon nutmeg
salt and freshly ground black pepper	salt and freshly ground black pepper
1 quantity basic crêpe batter (see preceding recipe)	1 quantity basic crêpe batter (see preceding recipe)
butter or oil for frying	butter or oil for frying

Wash the spinach, shake dry and cook without additional water in a covered pan over moderate heat until just tender. Drain well, chop and return to the pan with the butter and seasonings. Stir over moderate heat until all the water has evaporated. Chop very finely or liquidise. Mix the spinach with an equal quantity of pancake batter. Heat a little oil or butter in a frying pan and fry thin pancakes.

Note These spinach crêpes are often served rolled and sprinkled with grated Parmesan, or stuffed with a savoury mixture of chopped green pepper, skinned and chopped fresh tomatoes and peeled prawns.

OMELETTE A L'OSEILLE
Sorrel omelette

IMPERIAL/METRIC	AMERICAN
2 oz./50 g. butter	¼ cup butter
1 lb./450 g. sorrel or spinach	1 lb. sorrel or spinach
8 eggs	8 eggs
salt and pepper	salt and pepper

Illustrated on page 25

In a large omelette pan, melt the butter. Wash the sorrel and cook in the butter without additional water. Meanwhile beat the eggs lightly with 1 tablespoon cold water and seasoning to taste. Pour the eggs over the sorrel and stir briskly, lifting the edges to let the uncooked egg run underneath. When still soft and runny on top (*moelleux*), turn over from the handle side and fold onto a warm plate. Serves four as a supper dish, or two as a substantial meal.

OMELETTE LYONNAISE
Onion omelette

IMPERIAL/METRIC	AMERICAN
1 large onion	1 large onion
1 oz./25 g. butter	2 tablespoons butter
2 oz./50 g. lean ham, chopped	¼ cup chopped lean ham
5 eggs	5 eggs
2 tablespoons cream	3 tablespoons cream
salt and freshly ground black pepper	salt and freshly ground black pepper
	To serve
sprigs of watercress	sprigs of watercress

Slice the onion into very thin rings. Melt the butter in an omelette pan and gently fry the ham and onion rings until softened. Beat together the eggs, cream, salt and pepper. Pour this mixture over the onions and ham and cook gently until set. Fold the omelette in half and cut into two. Serve with sprigs of watercress.

Variation
OMELETTE PAYSANNE

This version is very popular with school children who will have to miss the main meal. Diced cooked potato, in a quantity proportionate to the heartiness of the appetite, is added to the pan with the ham and onion rings. Most children can make this for themselves by the time they are tall enough to reach the top of the stove.

OMELETTE A LA MERE POULARDE
Mother Poularde's omelette

This speciality of the Mont St. Michel in Brittany is more of a true omelette. The pan is rubbed with garlic, then greased with butter and a whisper of very finely pounded dried local herbs is added to the egg mixture before pouring into the pan. On the famous Mount omelettes are still cooked over an open fire at enormous cost for tourists but it is the garlic and herbs which do the trick.

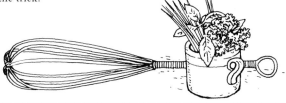

OEUFS MIRABEAU
Mirabeau eggs

IMPERIAL/METRIC	AMERICAN
8 eggs	8 eggs
6 tablespoons milk	½ cup milk
pinch grated nutmeg	pinch grated nutmeg
salt and pepper	salt and pepper
½ oz./15 g. butter	1 tablespoon butter
Tomato purée	
8 oz./225 g. fresh tomatoes	½ lb. fresh tomatoes
1 clove garlic, crushed	1 clove garlic, crushed
salt and freshly ground black pepper	salt and freshly ground black pepper
½ oz./15 g. butter	1 tablespoon butter

Beat together the eggs and add the milk, nutmeg and seasoning. Butter four individual cocotte dishes and pour in the egg mixture. Place the cocotte dishes in a roasting tin, half-filled with water. Cook in a moderately hot oven (375°F., 190°C., Gas Mark 5) for 20 minutes. To make the tomato purée, peel, deseed and chop the tomatoes. Put them in a small saucepan with the garlic and seasoning and simmer for 10 minutes. Pass through a fine sieve or liquidise and then sieve. Blend in the butter, check seasoning and reheat. Serve the oeufs mirabeau unmoulded and topped with the tomato purée.

Note This dish can also be served with a white sauce.

BEIGNETS MOUSSELINES
Cheese and ham fritters

IMPERIAL/METRIC	AMERICAN
½ pint/3 dl. oil for deep-frying	1¼ cups oil for deep-frying
2 oz./50 g. flour	½ cup flour
4 egg whites	4 egg whites
4 oz./100 g. Gruyère cheese, grated	1 cup grated Gruyère cheese
6 oz./175 g. lean ham, chopped	¾ cup lean chopped ham
salt and pepper	salt and pepper

Heat the oil to boiling. Sift the flour onto a flat plate. Whisk the egg whites very stiffly. Fold in the cheese, ham and seasoning. Dredge spoonfuls of the mixture in flour and carefully place them in the hot fat. Deep-fry until the fritters are golden brown. Drain on kitchen paper and serve immediately.

Note These beignets puff up during the cooking. It is best to avoid putting too many in the hot fat at once.

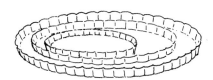

CROQUE MONSIEUR
Cheese savouries

IMPERIAL/METRIC	AMERICAN
8 slices bread (pain de mie)	8 slices bread (pain de mie)
2 oz./50 g. butter	¼ cup butter
4 thin slices Gruyère cheese	4 thin slices Gruyère cheese
4 slices lean ham	4 slices lean ham
1 tablespoon oil	1 tablespoon oil

Butter the bread and sandwich together with the cheese and ham. Heat the oil and remaining butter together in a large frying pan. Fry the sandwiches until golden brown on both sides. The cheese inside should be just soft and beginning to melt.

Note If all the sandwiches do not fit in the pan reserve part of the butter and oil for the second frying. Wipe out the pan with kitchen paper between batches. This is a cheap snack to ask for in a café when your supply of francs is nearly exhausted, but the bread will be toasted not fried.

LA GOYERE
Cheese tart

IMPERIAL/METRIC	AMERICAN
Pastry	
5 oz./150 g. plain flour	1¼ cups all-purpose flour
salt	salt
4 oz./110 g. butter	½ cup butter
Filling	
3 oz./75 g. curd cheese	⅓ cup curd cheese
2 oz./50 g. demi-sel cheese	¼ cup demi-sel cheese
1 large egg	1 large egg
4 tablespoons cream	⅓ cup cream
pinch pepper	pinch pepper

Sieve the flour with a pinch of salt and make into a paste with half the butter and a very little cold water. Roll out to an oblong ½ inch (1 cm.) thick, dot with half the remaining butter, fold in three, give a half turn and roll out again. Repeat the process with the last of the butter. Roll and fold once more, then allow the pastry to rest in a cold place for 1 hour. Mix the two cheeses together, beat in the egg, cream and pepper. Roll out the pastry thinly, use to line a greased 8-inch (20-cm.) flan tin, spread with the cheese mixture and bake in a moderate oven (350°F., 180°C., Gas Mark 4) for 30–35 minutes. Serve each portion hot with a nut of butter melting on top.

FLAMICHE
Leek flan

IMPERIAL/METRIC	AMERICAN
Pastry	
6 oz./175 g. plain flour	1½ cups all-purpose flour
4 oz./110 g. butter	½ cup butter
¼ teaspoon salt	¼ teaspoon salt
2 tablespoons cold water	3 tablespoons cold water
Filling	
1 oz./25 g. butter	2 tablespoons butter
2 oz./50 g. lean bacon, diced	¼ cup lean diced bacon
8 young leeks, thinly sliced	8 young leeks, thinly sliced
½ pint/3 dl. béchamel sauce (see page 66)	1¼ cups béchamel sauce (see page 66)
3 tablespoons single cream	¼ cup light cream
grated nutmeg	grated nutmeg
salt and pepper	salt and pepper
To serve	
green salad	green salad

Make up the pastry, roll out and use to line an 8-inch (20-cm.) flan tin. Allow to rest in the refrigerator for 30 minutes. Melt the butter in a heavy sauté pan and fry the bacon. Remove and keep warm. Add the leeks to the remaining fat and sauté gently until they are soft but not brown. Heat the sauce and stir in the leeks. Add the cream, bacon and seasonings. Mix thoroughly and pour into the prepared pastry case. Bake in a moderately hot oven (375°F., 190°C., Gas Mark 5) for 30–35 minutes. Serve hot with a green salad.

ENTREES

JAMBON AUX NOIX
Ham with walnuts

IMPERIAL/METRIC	AMERICAN
1½ oz./40 g. butter	3 tablespoons butter
4 thick slices ham	4 thick slices ham
1 oz./25 g. white breadcrumbs	½ cup white bread crumbs
2 oz./50 g. walnuts, chopped	½ cup chopped walnuts
2 tablespoons stock	3 tablespoons bouillon
2 tablespoons white Vermouth	3 tablespoons white Vermouth
salt and pepper	salt and pepper

Melt the butter in a heavy sauté pan and lightly fry the ham slices for 5 minutes on each side. Remove them from the pan and keep hot. Add the breadcrumbs and the walnuts to the hot butter and sauté until golden. Add the stock, Vermouth and seasonings and bring to a fast boil. Pour the sauce over the gammon and serve with *pommes de terre grillées*.

Note A dear old couple, who are relatives of mine *par affection* only, have just one item of produce from their tiny garden in Normandy to give away – nuts from their walnut tree. A kind daughter-in-law created this recipe to give them pleasure, as it does to all who taste it.

SAUCISSES AUX POMMES NORMANDES
Pork sausages with apples

IMPERIAL/METRIC	AMERICAN
1 oz./25 g. butter	2 tablespoons butter
1 lb./450 g. good pork sausages	1 lb. pork sausage links
4 large Golden Delicious apples	4 large Golden Delicious apples
2 tablespoons Calvados	3 tablespoons Calvados (applejack)

Melt the butter in a heavy frying pan. Prick the sausage skins with a fork and cook them gently in the melted butter for 10 minutes. Remove from the fat, drain them and arrange on a heated serving dish. Peel, core and slice the apples and fry them in the remaining butter until they are soft and golden. Place the apples round the sausages. Pour the warmed Calvados into the frying pan and ignite. Spoon the resulting juices over the sausages and apples and serve.

Note In Normandy this recipe is made with *andouilles*, a substantial smoked sausage, and large sweet Pommes Reinette apples, but personally I prefer it made with our own fresh pork sausages.

TRIPES AUX TOMATES
Tripe with tomatoes

IMPERIAL/METRIC	AMERICAN
2 lb./900 g. cooked tripe	2 lb. cooked tripe
seasoned flour	seasoned flour
1½ lb./675 g. tomatoes	1½ lb. tomatoes
2 large onions, sliced	2 large onions, sliced
1 clove garlic	1 clove garlic
3 tablespoons oil	¼ cup oil
¼ teaspoon ground cloves	¼ teaspoon ground cloves
1 tablespoon chopped parsley	1 tablespoon chopped parsley
salt and freshly ground white pepper	salt and freshly ground white pepper

Cut the tripe into thin strips and turn in the seasoned flour. Peel, deseed and chop the tomatoes. Sauté the onions and garlic in the oil until pale golden, add the tripe and sauté for 3 minutes, turning frequently. Add the tomatoes, cloves and parsley, stir well, cover and simmer for 15 minutes. Adjust the seasoning and serve with potatoes boiled *à l'anglaise*.

Note Tripe is far more popular in France than it is here but is rarely prepared at home *à la mode de Caen* because it is rather an elaborate recipe. The tripe is cooked with calves' feet (for many hours until the meat falls from the bones) with cider and Calvados. It is usually purchased fully prepared from a *charcuterie* and reheated at home.

PAIN D'AUBERGINES
Aubergine mould with savoury rice

IMPERIAL/METRIC	AMERICAN
6 oz./175 g. long-grain rice	scant cup long-grain rice
2 lb./900 g. tomatoes	2 lb. tomatoes
salt and freshly ground black pepper	salt and freshly ground black pepper
2 cloves garlic, crushed	2 cloves garlic, crushed
2 tablespoons fresh basil, chopped, or 2 teaspoons dried basil	3 tablespoons fresh basil, chopped, or 2 teaspoons dried basil
4 oz./100 g. fat bacon, diced	½ cup diced fat bacon
1½ lb./675 g. aubergines	1½ lb. eggplants
olive oil for frying	olive oil for frying
2 tablespoons chopped parsley	3 tablespoons chopped parsley
8 oz./225 g. Gruyère or Parmesan cheese, finely grated	2 cups finely grated Gruyère or Parmesan cheese
3 eggs	3 eggs

Cook the rice in salted water, drain well. Cook the peeled and deseeded tomatoes with salt, pepper, garlic and basil until soft. Fry the diced bacon gently to render out the fat. Slice the aubergines thinly lengthwise and fry in oil until just limp, then drain. Butter an 8-inch (20-cm.) mould, line it with overlapping aubergine slices. Blend the rice, tomato mixture, parsley, diced bacon, cheese and lightly beaten eggs. Turn into the mould, cover with more aubergine slices, then with a sheet of foil. Cook in the centre of a moderately hot oven (400°F., 200°C., Gas Mark 6) for 30 minutes. Cool slightly and turn out. Serve warm.

Illustrated on page 28

QUICHES DE FETE DE MADAME HOLLANDE
Madame Hollande's party quiches

IMPERIAL/METRIC	AMERICAN
Pâte brisée	
8 oz./225 g. plain flour	2 cups all-purpose flour
pinch salt	pinch salt
4 oz./100 g. butter	½ cup butter
1 egg	1 egg
3 tablespoons water	¼ cup water
Filling	
4 oz./100 g. smoked salmon trimmings	¼ lb. smoked salmon trimmings
8 oz./225 g. prawns, shelled	1⅓ cups shelled prawns
4 eggs	4 eggs
¾ pint/4 dl. milk	2 cups milk
¼ pint/1½ dl. cream	⅔ cup cream
salt and freshly ground white pepper	salt and freshly ground white pepper

Sift the flour and salt into a bowl, make a well in the centre, add butter, egg and water and work into a paste, gradually drawing in all the flour. Knead until smooth and silky. Wrap in foil and chill for 30 minutes. Roll out and use to line two quiche tins or fluted flan rings. Finely chop the small pieces of smoked salmon, removing any fragments of skin or bones, divide between the two flans, and sprinkle with prawns. Beat the eggs, milk, cream and seasoning together. Pour into the flans and bake in a moderately hot oven (375°F., 190°C., Gas Mark 5) for 25–30 minutes. Serve hot or cold.

Note As the proportion of egg in pâte brisée is important it is difficult to suggest making a small quantity for one flan only, but half a beaten egg can be used and the other ingredients halved easily. Madame Hollande cooks for my cousin Josette who thinks nothing of seating twenty guests at a family *réunion*, so her recipes tend to be for large quantities.

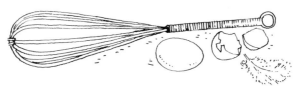

TOURTE A LA VIANDE
Yeast pastry meat pie

IMPERIAL/METRIC	AMERICAN
Yeast pastry	
1½ teaspoons dried yeast	1½ teaspoons active dry yeast
¼ pint/1½ dl. warm water	⅔ cup warm water
12 oz./350 g. strong plain flour	3 cups bread flour
½ teaspoon salt	½ teaspoon salt
4 oz./100 g. butter	½ cup butter
Filling	
2 oz./50 g. butter	¼ cup butter
2 lb./900 g. pie veal	2 lb. veal stewmeat
1 small onion, chopped	1 small onion, chopped
4 fl. oz./1 dl. white wine	1 cup white wine
1 teaspoon 'bouquet of herbs'	1 teaspoon 'bouquet of herbs'
salt and pepper	salt and pepper
12 oz./350 g. button mushrooms, chopped	3 cups chopped button mushrooms
1 tablespoon fine breadcrumbs	1 tablespoon fine bread crumbs

Sprinkle the yeast over the warm water in a jug and leave until frothy, about 10 minutes. Sieve together the flour and salt. Add the butter, softened but not melted, pour in the yeast mixture and stir with your hand until it forms a ball of soft dough. Allow to stand. To make the filling, melt the butter in a cocotte, turn the diced meat in it until pale golden and add the onion, wine and seasonings. Cover and simmer for 35 minutes, then add the mushrooms and cook for another 20 minutes. Strain off the juices and reduce if necessary to ¼ pint (1½ dl., ⅔ cup), then thicken with the breadcrumbs. Mix with the meat and mushrooms. Grease a tourte mould, roll out two-thirds of the pastry and use to line the mould. Fill with meat mixture, roll out the remaining pastry and use to cover. Make a steam vent and bake in a moderately hot oven (375°F., 190°C., Gas Mark 5) until golden brown, about 40 minutes. Serve hot.

Illustrated on page 29

Note This is a big tourte which serves six people amply, but the recipe is not so successful with a smaller one.

PAUPIETTES D'AGNEAU
Stuffed lamb rolls

IMPERIAL/METRIC	AMERICAN
4 fillets lean lamb (cut from the leg)	4 lamb leg steaks
2 oz./50 g. sausage meat	$\frac{1}{4}$ cup sausage meat
2 oz./50 g. thinly sliced ham, chopped	$\frac{1}{4}$ cup chopped ham
2 oz./50 g. lean bacon, chopped	$\frac{1}{4}$ cup chopped lean bacon
1 tablespoon chopped parsley	1 tablespoon chopped parsley
1 clove garlic, crushed	1 clove garlic, crushed
salt and pepper	salt and pepper
1 egg yolk, beaten	1 egg yolk, beaten
oil	oil
2 oz./50 g. fresh breadcrumbs	$\frac{1}{2}$ cup fresh bread crumbs

Ask the butcher to 'bat' the fillets very flat. Trim them square. Mix together the sausage meat, ham and bacon. Add the parsley, garlic and seasonings and bind with the egg yolk. Spread the stuffing over the fillets. Roll them up and secure with strong thread in two places. Brush the rolls with oil, sprinkle with breadcrumbs and cook under a medium grill for 20 minutes. Turn once during the cooking time. Remove threads and serve with a green salad.

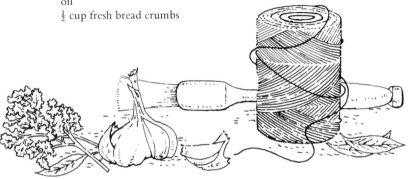

GRATIN D'AGNEAU
Country-style lamb

IMPERIAL/METRIC	AMERICAN
1 oz./25 g. butter	2 tablespoons butter
1 tablespoon oil	1 tablespoon oil
4 shallots, chopped	4 shallots, chopped
1 lb./450 g. cooked lamb, minced	1 lb. cooked lamb, ground
1 clove garlic, crushed	1 clove garlic, crushed
salt and pepper	salt and pepper
2 turnips, diced	2 turnips, diced
2 tablespoons fresh breadcrumbs	3 tablespoons fresh bread crumbs
1 oz./25 g. cheese, grated	$\frac{1}{4}$ cup grated cheese

Heat half the butter and the oil in a heavy frying pan. Sauté the shallots gently until soft. Add the minced lamb, garlic and seasonings. Transfer the mixture to a shallow ovenproof dish. Meanwhile, boil the turnips in salted water for 20 minutes. Drain them and pass through a sieve. Mix the resulting purée with the breadcrumbs and spread it over the meat. Sprinkle with cheese, dot with butter and brown in a moderately hot oven (375°F., 190°C., Gas Mark 5) for 20 minutes.

Note This is really a continental shepherd's pie, and ideal for using up leftovers. The turnip topping instead of potatoes gives a much lighter and more interesting finish.

MEAT, POULTRY AND GAME

COTELETTES DE VEAU FLAMBEES
Flambéed veal cutlets

IMPERIAL/METRIC	AMERICAN
2 oz./50 g. butter	$\frac{1}{4}$ cup butter
4 veal cutlets	4 veal chops
8 oz./225 g. mushrooms, chopped	2 cups chopped mushrooms
2 tablespoons chopped parsley	3 tablespoons chopped parsley
1 teaspoon chopped tarragon	1 teaspoon chopped tarragon
2 tablespoons Pernod	3 tablespoons Pernod
$\frac{1}{4}$ pint/1$\frac{1}{2}$ dl. double cream	$\frac{2}{3}$ cup heavy cream

Heat the butter in a frying pan and brown the cutlets on both sides. Add the mushrooms and herbs and continue cooking gently for 5 minutes. Pour the warmed Pernod over the meat and ignite. Transfer the cutlets and mushrooms to a serving dish and keep warm. Bring the pan juices to the boil and then stir in the cream. Heat the sauce through, being careful not to let it boil, and pour over the veal. (Vodka makes a surprisingly good substitute for Pernod if you cannot get it.)

ESCALOPES DE VEAU EN PAPILLOTE
Veal escalopes in parcels

IMPERIAL/METRIC	AMERICAN
4 4-oz./100-g. veal escalopes	4 $\frac{1}{4}$-lb. veal cutlets
2 oz./50 g. butter	$\frac{1}{4}$ cup butter
salt and freshly ground white pepper	salt and freshly ground white pepper
4 shallots, chopped	4 shallots, chopped
8 oz./225 g. mushrooms, chopped	2 cups chopped mushrooms
1 tablespoon chopped parsley	1 tablespoon chopped parsley
4 slices lean ham	4 slices lean ham

Ask the butcher to 'bat' the escalopes well. Melt most of the butter in a heavy sauté pan. Season the escalopes and fry them quickly on both sides. Cut out four heart-shaped pieces of greaseproof paper. Butter one half of each heart and place the prepared escalope on top. Fry the shallots and mushrooms in the sauté pan previously used for the meat. Add more butter if necessary. Blend in the parsley when the vegetables are soft. Spread the mixture on each escalope and top each with a slice of ham. Cover with the unbuttered half of each 'heart' and roll in all edges to seal. Cook on a baking sheet in a moderately hot oven (400°F., 200°C., Gas Mark 6) for 25 minutes.

Note Using greaseproof paper is the traditional French method for this recipe but it is much easier to crimp together the edges of foil (see step-by-step line drawings opposite).

ROTI DE PORC AU ROMARIN
Roast pork with rosemary

IMPERIAL/METRIC	AMERICAN
1 pint/6 dl. cider vinegar	2½ cups cider vinegar
1 bunch rosemary	1 bunch rosemary
2 large onions	2 large onions
2 cloves	2 cloves
4 cloves garlic	4 cloves garlic
2 lb./900 g. loin of pork, boned and rolled	2 lb. boned and rolled pork loin roast
2 lb./900 g. courgettes, sliced	2 lb. zucchini, sliced
salt and freshly ground black pepper	salt and freshly ground black pepper
2 tablespoons oil	3 tablespoons oil

Heat the vinegar with ½ pint (3 dl., 1¼ cups) water, a sprig of rosemary, the onions stuck with cloves and one crushed clove of garlic. Cool. (As rosemary is very strongly flavoured use as much as suits your family's taste.) Spike the joint with tiny rosemary sprigs and slivers of garlic, using about 2 cloves. Put the joint into the cold marinade. Leave to marinate for 4–6 hours. Drain and roast for 2 hours in a moderate oven (350°F., 180°C., Gas Mark 4), basting with the marinade. Put the sliced courgettes in a small ovenproof dish, in layers. Add salt, pepper and a suspicion of chopped garlic and rosemary to each layer. When the dish is full, add 4 tablespoons of the marinade, and the oil, and cover. Cook at the same time as the meat, in the coolest part of the oven. To serve, strain the juices from the roasting pan over the pork and surround with courgettes.

FILET DE PORC EN CROUTE
Pork fillet in pastry

IMPERIAL/METRIC	AMERICAN
1 lb./450 g. pork fillet	1 lb. pork tenderloin
1 oz./25 g. butter	2 tablespoons butter
1 oz./25 g. liver pâté	2 tablespoons liver pâté
1 lb./450 g. puff pastry	1 lb. puff paste
1 egg	1 egg
Duxelles	
2 oz./50 g. butter	¼ cup butter
12 oz./350 g. mushrooms, chopped	3 cups chopped mushrooms
2 oz./50 g. lean ham, chopped	¼ cup lean chopped ham
1 onion, chopped	1 onion, chopped
salt and pepper	salt and pepper
1 sprig thyme, chopped	1 sprig thyme, chopped
2 eggs	2 eggs
1 tablespoon fresh breadcrumbs	1 tablespoon fresh bread crumbs
2 tablespoons chopped parsley	3 tablespoons chopped parsley

Trim the pork and cut off any fat. Melt the butter in a heavy frying pan and sear the meat all over. Remove from the pan and allow to cool. Make up the duxelles as follows. Heat the butter and gently fry the mushrooms, ham and onion for 5 minutes. Remove from the heat and add salt, pepper and thyme. Beat the eggs and fold them with the breadcrumbs and parsley into the prepared mixture. Cook carefully, stirring all the time, for 3 minutes, then leave to cool. Spread the fillet with pâté and season well. Roll out the puff pastry. Place the fillet in the centre and cover with the duxelles. Wrap the pastry firmly round the fillet and seal neatly. Place on a damped baking sheet with the join underneath. Brush the pastry with beaten egg and prick lightly with a fork. Bake in a hot oven (450°F., 230°C., Gas Mark 8) for 20–30 minutes.

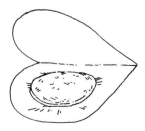

NOISETTES D'AGNEAU EN BROCHETTE
Skewered noisettes of lamb

IMPERIAL/METRIC	AMERICAN
8 lamb cutlets	8 lamb rib chops
4 small firm tomatoes	4 small firm tomatoes
2 courgettes	2 zucchini
4 oz./100 g. lean bacon, diced	½ cup lean diced bacon
4 bay leaves	4 bay leaves
1 tablespoon oil	1 tablespoon oil
1 tablespoon lemon juice	1 tablespoon lemon juice
salt and pepper	salt and pepper

Trim off any bone and fat from the cutlets and dice the remaining meat. Halve the tomatoes and slice the courgettes into 1-inch (2-cm.) pieces. Place the lamb, bacon and vegetables alternately on four skewers with a bay leaf in the centre. Brush with oil and sprinkle with lemon juice. Season and grill for 10 minutes. Turn frequently. Serve with saffron rice, which can be cooked while the skewers are prepared and grilled.

Note If time permits, make a marinade with the oil, lemon juice, bay leaves and seasoning a couple of hours beforehand and marinate the diced lamb in this. A sprig of fresh rosemary improves the marinade.

LAPIN A LA MOUTARDE
Rabbit in mustard sauce

IMPERIAL/METRIC	AMERICAN
1 plump rabbit, jointed	1 plump rabbit, jointed
3 tablespoons oil	¼ cup oil
4 tablespoons Dijon mustard	⅓ cup Dijon mustard
bouquet garni	bouquet garni
¼ pint/1½ dl. cream	⅔ cup cream
salt and freshly ground black pepper	salt and freshly ground black pepper

Turn the rabbit joints in the hot oil until golden, add the mustard and bouquet garni and stir well. Cover and cook gently for 15 minutes. Add the cream and 2 tablespoons water. Cover and simmer for 40 minutes, or until the rabbit is tender. Remove the bouquet garni and adjust the seasoning. Serve with plenty of potatoes.

Note A method favoured in Northern France is to roast the rabbit, the joints well coated with mustard then wrapped in thin slices of fat bacon, for 1 hour. The pan juices are poured over boiled potatoes cooked *à l'anglaise*.

CANETON A LA CHOUCROUTE
Duckling with sauerkraut

IMPERIAL/METRIC	AMERICAN
1 4½- to 5-lb./2- to 2¼-kg. duckling	1 4½- to 5-lb. duckling
salt and freshly ground white pepper	salt and freshly ground white pepper
¼ pint/1½ dl. Riesling or other dry white wine	⅔ cup Riesling or other dry white wine
2 bay leaves	2 bay leaves
2 lb./900 g. sauerkraut	2 lb. sauerkraut
1 oz./25 g. flour	¼ cup flour
2 teaspoons sugar	2 teaspoons sugar

Sprinkle the duck with salt and pepper inside and out. Roast in a moderately hot oven (400°F., 200°C., Gas Mark 6) for 1 hour 20 minutes, or a little longer for a large duckling. Remove from the tin, strain all the fat into a jug and reserve. Boil the wine, with the bay leaves, over high heat for a few minutes to reduce by half. Put the sauerkraut in an ovenproof casserole. (If canned it must be very well drained.) Blend the flour into 2 tablespoons of the hot duck fat, add the reduced wine and the sugar and mix well. Stir into the sauerkraut and put the covered casserole into the oven for 5 minutes. Meanwhile carve the duck into serving portions. Arrange on the bed of sauerkraut, cover and return to the oven for 30 minutes. Serve with boiled potatoes.

Note This is the only one of my family recipes which came straight to me, via my mother, from my grandfather who was born in Strasbourg. She remembered he always had it on his birthday.

POULET EN MATELOTE
Chicken in cream sauce

IMPERIAL/METRIC	AMERICAN
1 large roasting chicken	1 large roasting chicken
1 tablespoon seasoned flour	1 tablespoon seasoned flour
4 oz./100 g. butter	$\frac{1}{2}$ cup butter
2 tablespoons brandy	3 tablespoons brandy
2 shallots, chopped	2 shallots, chopped
bouquet garni	bouquet garni
salt and pepper	salt and pepper
1 pint/6 dl. dry white wine	$2\frac{1}{2}$ cups dry white wine
$\frac{1}{4}$ pint/1$\frac{1}{2}$ dl. cream	$\frac{2}{3}$ cup heavy cream
2 tablespoons chopped parsley and chervil	3 tablespoons chopped parsley and chervil

Joint the chicken, turn in seasoned flour and sauté in the butter until pale golden. Ignite the warm brandy and pour over the chicken. Add the shallots, bouquet garni, salt, pepper and wine. Cook, uncovered, until the chicken is tender, about 40 minutes. Lightly whip the cream, stir in the fresh herbs, strain over this the juices from the pan and stir again. Pour over the chicken portions and reheat carefully without boiling.

Illustrated on page 52

POULET A LA VALLEE D'AUGE
Chicken in Normandy style

IMPERIAL/METRIC	AMERICAN
1 plump chicken, about 3$\frac{1}{2}$ lb./1$\frac{1}{2}$ kg.	1 plump chicken, about 3$\frac{1}{2}$ lb.
3 oz./75 g. butter	6 tablespoons butter
1 tablespoon oil	1 tablespoon oil
1 tablespoon flour	1 tablespoon flour
2 tablespoons Calvados	3 tablespoons Calvados or applejack
$\frac{1}{4}$ pint/1$\frac{1}{2}$ dl. dry cider	$\frac{2}{3}$ cup dry cider
$\frac{1}{4}$ pint/1$\frac{1}{2}$ dl. chicken stock	$\frac{2}{3}$ cup chicken bouillon
bouquet garni	bouquet garni
salt and freshly ground white pepper	salt and freshly ground white pepper
5 dessert apples, French Pommes Reinette or Golden Delicious	5 dessert apples, Golden Delicious or McIntosh
$\frac{1}{4}$ pint/1$\frac{1}{2}$ dl. cream	$\frac{2}{3}$ cup cream

Joint the chicken. Heat 1 oz. (25 g., 2 tablespoons) of the butter and the oil in a flameproof casserole and brown the chicken portions. Sprinkle in the flour and stir well. Warm the Calvados in a ladle, ignite and pour over the chicken. Add the cider, stock, bouquet garni and seasoning to taste. Peel, core and chop two of the apples and add to the casserole. Cover and cook in a moderately hot oven (375°F., 190°C., Gas Mark 5) for 45 minutes. Meanwhile, peel, core and quarter the remaining apples and fry in the remaining butter until golden brown. Remove the chicken portions to a serving dish, sieve the contents of the casserole, bring to the boil again and boil rapidly for 2 minutes to reduce. Adjust seasoning and add the cream. Reheat gently without boiling. Pour over the chicken and serve garnished with the fried apple quarters.

ROGNONS A LA BOURGUIGNONNE
Lambs' kidneys in Burgundy

IMPERIAL/METRIC	AMERICAN
1 oz./25 g. butter	2 tablespoons butter
1 tablespoon oil	1 tablespoon oil
1 onion, chopped	1 onion, chopped
4 oz./100 g. mushrooms, chopped	1 cup chopped mushrooms
4 oz./100 g. fat green bacon, diced	$\frac{1}{2}$ cup diced unsmoked bacon
8 lambs' kidneys	8 lamb kidneys
$\frac{1}{2}$ pint/3 dl. dry red wine	$1\frac{1}{4}$ cups dry red wine
salt and pepper	salt and pepper
1 clove garlic, crushed	1 clove garlic, crushed
bouquet garni	bouquet garni
1 tablespoon flour	1 tablespoon flour
1 tablespoon chopped parsley	1 tablespoon chopped parsley

Heat half the butter and the oil in a heavy frying pan. Sauté the onion, mushrooms and bacon gently then remove from the fat and keep warm. Split the kidneys in half, remove the cores and just brown in the butter and oil. Transfer to a serving dish and keep hot. Add the wine to the frying pan and return the onion, mushroom and bacon mixture. Add the seasonings, garlic and bouquet garni. Simmer for 10 minutes. Prepare a *beurre manié* with the remaining butter and the flour and use to thicken the sauce. Pour the sauce over the kidneys and serve sprinkled with chopped parsley.

Note As the title suggests, the wine used in this recipe should be a mature full-bodied red wine. As the recipe takes only a short time to cook, the bottle should have been opened in advance to let the wine 'breathe' before serving at table; a litre bottle provides sufficient for this dish and for five or six glasses.

LANGUE DE BOEUF AUX MARRONS
Tongue with chestnuts

IMPERIAL/METRIC	AMERICAN
1 ox tongue, about 4 lb./2 kg.	1 beef tongue, about 4 lb.
2 carrots	2 carrots
2 onions, stuck with 4 cloves	2 onions, stuck with 4 cloves
bouquet garni	bouquet garni
$\frac{1}{4}$ pint/1$\frac{1}{2}$ dl. dry or draught cider	$\frac{2}{3}$ cup dry or draught cider
1 lb./450 g. chestnuts	1 lb. chestnuts
$\frac{1}{2}$ oz./15 g. butter	1 tablespoon butter
salt and freshly ground black pepper	salt and freshly ground black pepper
1 teaspoon ground coriander	1 teaspoon ground coriander

Soak the tongue in cold water overnight. Put it in a pan with fresh water to cover, the sliced carrots, onions and bouquet garni. Bring to the boil, skim and simmer for 3 hours. Drain, skin and trim away small bones at the root. Put the tongue into an ovenproof casserole which it just fits, add the cider and just enough of the strained stock to cover. Cook in a moderate oven (350°F., 180°C., Gas Mark 4) for 1 hour. Meanwhile, boil the chestnuts for 20 minutes, peel and sieve. Beat in the butter, seasoning and spice. Serve the tongue thickly sliced on a bed of chestnut purée, masked with sauce Espagnole or Madère (see page 66).

CASSEROLES

NAVARIN PRINTANIER
Spring lamb casserole

IMPERIAL/METRIC	AMERICAN
3 lb./1½ kg. lean shoulder of lamb, boned	3 lb. lean lamb shoulder, boned
2 oz./50 g. butter	¼ cup butter
3 shallots, chopped	3 shallots, chopped
1 clove garlic, crushed	1 clove garlic, crushed
2 oz./50 g. flour	½ cup flour
1 pint/6 dl. hot stock	2½ cups hot bouillon
salt and freshly ground black pepper	salt and freshly ground black pepper
bouquet garni	bouquet garni
1 lb./450 g. baby new potatoes	1 lb. baby new potatoes
8 oz./225 g. small carrots	½ lb. small carrots
4 small turnips	4 small turnips
1 lb./450 g. fresh peas	1 lb. fresh peas
chopped parsley	chopped parsley

Cube the meat. Heat the butter in a flameproof casserole and brown the shallots, garlic and meat together. Remove them from the fat and keep warm. Blend the flour into the remaining fat in the casserole and gradually add the stock. Bring to the boil, stirring constantly. Return the shallots, garlic and meat and add the seasonings and bouquet garni. Cover and cook in a moderate oven (325°F., 170°C., Gas Mark 3) for 1 hour. Peel the potatoes, dice the carrots and quarter the turnips. Add to the navarin and continue cooking for a further 40 minutes. Shell the peas and add them to the casserole for the last 10 minutes. Remove the bouquet garni and serve the navarin sprinkled with parsley.

Note This is traditionally served as soon as the first baby vegetables appear in the local market. My cousins who live in the same town vie with each other to be first to get it on the family table.

BOEUF EN DAUBE
Beef stewed in red wine

A *daubière* is an earthenware casserole in which beef is stewed with very little liquid at a low temperature for many hours, until it is tender enough to be eaten with a spoon. The cut is not important, but the marinading of the meat and the airtight seal of the casserole are essential. The marinade should contain red wine, olive oil, garlic, herbs and spices to *daubière* with the strained marinade. Put into a very, very slow oven and forget it, overnight if possible and if the heat is low enough. Unless the seal is perfect, make up a strip of flour-and-water dough and press round the edge before putting on the lid firmly.

POT-AU-FEU BRETON
Breton stew

IMPERIAL/METRIC	AMERICAN
3 lb./1¼ kg. silverside	3 lb. rolled rump
1 lb./450 g. knuckle of veal	1 lb. veal foreshank
1½ teaspoons salt	1½ teaspoons salt
½ teaspoon freshly ground black pepper	½ teaspoon freshly ground black pepper
2 onions	2 onions
3 carrots	3 carrots
2 leeks, trimmed	2 leeks, trimmed
2 lb./900 g. Savoy cabbage	2 lb. Savoy cabbage
2 cloves	2 cloves
bouquet garni	bouquet garni

Tie the beef into shape and put with the knuckle of veal into a large casserole with the salt, pepper and 5–6 pints (3 litres, 6–7 pints) water. Bring to the boil, skim and simmer gently, covered, for 1 hour. Halve the onions, slice the carrots and leeks lengthwise, quarter the cabbage. Wash all the vegetables, stick the onions with the cloves and add prepared vegetables to the pot, with the bouquet garni. Bring to the boil, skim, cover and simmer for 2½–3 hours.

Illustrated opposite

Le bouilli Serve the beef neatly sliced, with the meat from the veal knuckle and the vegetables, on a warmed platter, slightly moistened with the bouillon and accompanied by plain boiled potatoes, gherkins and sweet pickles.

Le bouillon Strain the broth, allow to get cold, remove fat, reheat and serve next day with bread. The remaining meat can be served as a salad.

Viande de pot-au-feu en salade Chop the cooked meat finely. Mix with cubed cooked beetroot, chopped celery heart, mild onion and a few shallots, 1 tablespoon each chopped parsley, chervil and capers. Make a dressing with pounded yolk of hard-boiled egg, Dijon mustard, salt, black pepper, wine vinegar and salt. Arrange the salad in a bowl on a bed of lettuce leaves, pour over the dressing.

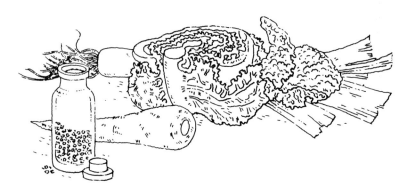

CASSEROLE DE BOEUF DAUPHINOISE
Beef dauphinoise

IMPERIAL/METRIC	AMERICAN
1½ oz./40 g. butter	3 tablespoons butter
3 tablespoons oil	¼ cup oil
4 thin rump steaks	4 thin top round steaks
1 onion, sliced	1 onion, sliced
2 shallots, sliced	2 shallots, sliced
4 anchovy fillets	4 anchovy fillets
1 oz./25 g. flour	¼ cup flour
2 cloves garlic, crushed	2 cloves garlic, crushed
1 tablespoon wine vinegar	1 tablespoon wine vinegar
2 tablespoons chopped parsley	3 tablespoons chopped parsley
salt and pepper	salt and pepper

Heat the butter and 1 tablespoon oil in a heavy frying pan. Brown the steaks quickly on both sides. Remove them from the pan and keep warm. Sauté the onion and shallots in the fat remaining in the pan. Place half the onion mixture in the bottom of a shallow ovenproof dish. Put the steaks on top and cover with the rest of the onions and shallots. Pound together the anchovy fillets, remaining oil, flour, garlic, vinegar, parsley, salt and pepper. Blend until smooth. Cover the onions with the paste and cook, covered, in a moderate oven (350°F., 180°C., Gas Mark 4) for 30 minutes.

Pot-au-feu Breton (page 48)

BOEUF A LA PROVENCALE
Provençale beef

IMPERIAL/METRIC	AMERICAN
2 tablespoons oil	3 tablespoons oil
4 oz./100 g. bacon, diced	$\frac{1}{2}$ cup diced bacon
1 onion, quartered	1 onion, quartered
4 shallots, chopped	4 shallots, chopped
2$\frac{1}{2}$ lb./generous kg. beef topside	2$\frac{1}{2}$ lb. beef round
salt and pepper	salt and pepper
4 tomatoes	4 tomatoes
1 carrot, chopped	1 carrot, chopped
2 cloves garlic, crushed	2 cloves garlic, crushed
bouquet garni	bouquet garni
8 tablespoons red wine	$\frac{2}{3}$ cup red wine
2 oz./50 g. black olives	$\frac{1}{3}$ cup ripe olives
2 oz./50 g. green olives	$\frac{1}{3}$ cup green olives

Heat the oil in a heavy frying pan and sauté the bacon, onion and shallots until golden. Remove from the pan and place in an earthenware casserole. Sear the meat quickly in the oil remaining in the pan and add to the casserole. Season well. Peel, deseed and roughly chop the tomatoes. Add to the casserole with the carrot, garlic and bouquet garni. Pour over the wine and cover closely. Cook in a cool oven (300°F., 150°C., Gas Mark 2) for 3 hours. Remove from the oven, skim the fat from the surface and check seasoning. Add the olives and continue cooking for a further 30 minutes.

BLANQUETTE DE VEAU GRAND'MERE
Granny's veal stew

IMPERIAL/METRIC	AMERICAN
2$\frac{1}{2}$ lb./generous kg. neck of veal	2$\frac{1}{2}$ lb. veal shoulder
2 oz./50 g. butter	$\frac{1}{4}$ cup butter
6 new carrots, sliced	6 new carrots, sliced
2 baby turnips, sliced	2 baby turnips, sliced
$\frac{1}{4}$ pint/1$\frac{1}{2}$ dl. dry white wine	$\frac{2}{3}$ cup dry white wine
$\frac{1}{2}$ teaspoon salt	$\frac{1}{2}$ teaspoon salt
$\frac{1}{4}$ teaspoon freshly ground white pepper	$\frac{1}{4}$ teaspoon freshly ground white pepper
2 lb./900 g. small new potatoes, peeled	2 lb. small new potatoes, peeled
2 tablespoons chopped tarragon	3 tablespoons chopped tarragon
4 tablespoons cream	$\frac{1}{3}$ cup cream

Chop the meat into neat portions. Melt the butter in a flameproof casserole and sauté the meat until sealed and pale golden, then add the carrots and turnips. Pour over the wine and sufficient water just to come through. Season to taste and cook, covered, for 45 minutes. Add the whole potatoes, re-cover and continue cooking until they are tender, about 30 minutes. Nearly all the liquid should be absorbed. Just before serving, stir the tarragon into the cream and spoon over the casserole.

LAPEREAU AUX OIGNONS
Young rabbit with onions

IMPERIAL/METRIC	AMERICAN
1 large bunch spring onions	1 large bunch scallions
1 large young rabbit	1 large young rabbit
4 oz./100 g. butter	$\frac{1}{2}$ cup butter
2 bay leaves	2 bay leaves
1 sprig thyme	1 sprig thyme
salt and freshly ground white pepper	salt and freshly ground white pepper
2 tomatoes	2 tomatoes
4 fl. oz./1 dl. dry white wine	$\frac{1}{2}$ cup dry white wine
3 tablespoons stock	$\frac{1}{4}$ cup bouillon

Trim the onions. Skin the rabbit and joint into convenient portions. Melt the butter, turn the rabbit joints in it until golden brown. Add the onions, bay leaves, thyme and salt and pepper to taste. Peel and deseed the tomatoes, stir into the pan, then pour over the wine and stock. Half cover and simmer for 30 minutes, so that the liquid partially evaporates, until the rabbit joints are tender. Serve very hot.

Illustrated on page 53

LIEVRE EN ETOUFFADE
Baked hare

IMPERIAL/METRIC	AMERICAN
1 tablespoon oil	1 tablespoon oil
1 lb./450 g. sausage meat	2 cups sausage meat
1 onion, chopped	1 onion, chopped
4 oz./100 g. fat bacon, diced	½ cup diced fat bacon
1 young hare, jointed	1 young hare, jointed
salt and pepper	salt and pepper
bouquet garni	bouquet garni
8 tablespoons white wine	⅔ cup white wine
4 rashers fat bacon	4 slices fat bacon

Brush a heavy casserole with oil. Spread the sausage meat over the bottom of the pot. Lay the onion, bacon pieces and hare joints on the sausage meat. Season and add the bouquet garni. Moisten with the wine and top with the bacon rashers. Cover closely and cook in a moderate oven (325°F., 170°C., Gas Mark 3) for 2 hours.

Note This dish can also be served cold with a green salad.

LA POULE AU POT
Chicken in the pot

IMPERIAL/METRIC	AMERICAN
1 3- to 3½-lb./1¼- to 1½-kg. chicken	1 3- to 3½-lb. chicken
3 carrots, chopped	3 carrots, chopped
1 stalk celery, chopped	1 stalk celery, chopped
1 leek, sliced	1 leek, sliced
2 small turnips, quartered	2 small turnips, quartered
salt and pepper	salt and pepper
bouquet garni	bouquet garni

Stuffing

IMPERIAL/METRIC	AMERICAN
liver of the chicken	liver of the chicken
4 oz./100 g. green bacon	5 slices unsmoked bacon
2 cloves garlic, crushed	2 cloves garlic, crushed
4 oz./100 g. minced pork	½ cup ground pork
2 tablespoons finely chopped parsley	3 tablespoons finely chopped parsley
¼ teaspoon nutmeg	¼ teaspoon nutmeg
salt and pepper	salt and pepper
2 shallots, chopped	2 shallots, chopped
4 oz./100 g. stale breadcrumbs	1 cup stale bread crumbs
¼ pint/1½ dl. milk	⅔ cup milk
2 eggs, beaten	2 eggs, beaten

To make the stuffing, mince together the chicken liver and green bacon. Add the garlic, minced pork, parsley, nutmeg, seasoning and shallots. Moisten the breadcrumbs with the milk, add the eggs and stir into the meat mixture. Stuff the chicken and sew up tightly. Place the bird in a large saucepan with 3 pints (1¾ litres, 2 quarts) boiling water. Add the vegetables, seasoning and bouquet garni and cook gently for 1½ hours. Drain the chicken, place on a warm serving dish and keep hot. Strain the stock and serve first as a clear soup. Serve the chicken afterwards, surrounded with freshly cooked vegetables.

Poulet en matelote (page 45)

Lapereau aux oignons (page 50)

VEGETABLES

POMMES DE TERRE
Potatoes

Pommes de terre Anna Peel floury potatoes and slice thickly, arrange in a thickly buttered shallow casserole, overlapping in layers. Sprinkle each layer with salt, a dash of freshly ground pepper, and some tiny nuts of butter. Cover and bake in a moderate oven (350°F., 180°C., Gas Mark 4) for 40 minutes. Remove cover and turn out like a gâteau, easing it out with a palette knife.

Pommes de terre fondantes Peel 1 lb. (450 g.) floury potatoes and slice thickly, plunge into boiling salted water and boil for 3 minutes then drain. Butter a shallow casserole well. Melt 4 oz. (100 g., $\frac{1}{2}$ cup) butter with 3 tablespoons of the salted water used for cooking the potatoes. Arrange a layer of potato slices in the casserole, sprinkle with salt, a dash of freshly ground pepper and about a tablespoon of the melted butter mixture. Continue adding to the layers until all are used, ending with butter mixture. Cover and bake in a moderate oven (350°F., 180°C., Gas Mark 4) for 15 minutes, then remove the cover. As the water evaporates the potatoes become golden in colour. Serve when tender.

Pommes de terre Dauphine Cook 1 lb. (450 g.) even-sized floury potatoes, unpeeled, in boiling salted water. Cool and peel, then sieve. Make up a batch of choux paste based on 3 eggs (see page 75), beat in an extra egg, then beat in the sieved potatoes. Chill the mixture. Heat cooking oil until a cube of bread frizzles at once when added, then drop in spoonfuls of the paste. Fry until golden, remove with draining spoon onto kitchen paper and serve hot. An alternative method is to omit the extra egg, making the mixture stiffer, and pipe onto a greased baking tray. Brush with egg wash and bake in a moderately hot oven (375°F., 190°C., Gas Mark 5) for 25 minutes, or until golden brown.

Note To avoid confusing this recipe with gratin à la dauphinoise, remember that the latter is the style of cooking peculiar to Dauphiné, the former a dish dedicated by a chef to the then Dauphine of France.

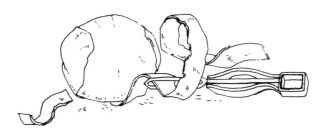

GRATIN A LA DAUPHINOISE
Potatoes baked with cream

IMPERIAL/METRIC	AMERICAN
1½ oz./40 g. butter	3 tablespoons butter
1 clove garlic, crushed	1 clove garlic, crushed
salt and pepper	salt and pepper
1 lb./450 g. new potatoes	1 lb. new potatoes
¼ pint/1½ dl. cream	⅔ cup heavy cream
6 oz./175 g. Gruyère cheese, grated	1½ cups grated Gruyère cheese
¼ teaspoon grated nutmeg	¼ teaspoon grated nutmeg

Pound together the butter and garlic. Add salt and pepper and use half to grease a shallow ovenproof dish. Peel the potatoes and slice thinly. Leave them to soak in cold water for a few minutes, then drain and dry them thoroughly. Arrange half the potatoes in the prepared dish, pour over half the cream and sprinkle over half the grated cheese. Season well with salt, pepper and nutmeg and dot with more butter/garlic mixture. Place the remaining potatoes evenly on top, pour over the rest of the cream and cover with the remaining cheese. Dot with the remaining garlic butter and cook in a moderate oven (350°F., 180°C., Gas Mark 4) for about 45 minutes.

Note Although always so named, the recipe is elaborated in other regions. Sometimes the casserole is merely rubbed round with a cut clove of garlic first, and the cream is replaced with an equal quantity of milk, lightly beaten with 1 egg.

FENOUIL MEUNIERE
Braised fennel

IMPERIAL/METRIC	AMERICAN
6 heads fennel	6 bulbs Florence fennel
1 lemon	1 lemon
4 oz./100 g. butter	½ cup butter
salt and freshly ground pepper	salt and freshly ground pepper
2 tablespoons chopped parsley	3 tablespoons chopped parsley

Remove the outside leaves and trim the base of the fennel. Wash thoroughly and put with the juice of the lemon into just sufficient lightly salted water to cover. Bring to the boil and simmer, covered, until just tender, but still very firm, about 20 minutes. Drain, cut each head in two, and arrange, cut surfaces down, in a well buttered ovenproof dish, sprinkling over the remaining butter, melted, and a good grind of pepper. Cook in a moderate oven (325°F., 170°C., Gas Mark 3) for 30 minutes. Baste several times, to impregnate the fennel with the butter. Serve sprinkled with the parsley. The slightly sweet *anis* flavour is superb.

Note Small heads of celery can be cooked in the same way.

PETITS POIS A LA FRANCAISE
Garden peas French style

IMPERIAL/METRIC	AMERICAN
2 oz./50 g. butter	¼ cup butter
3 shallots, chopped	3 shallots, chopped
1 lettuce, shredded	1 lettuce, shredded
1 lb./450 g. shelled small garden peas	1 lb. shelled small garden peas
salt	salt
1 teaspoon sugar	1 teaspoon sugar
thyme	thyme

Melt the butter in a heavy sauté pan. Add the shallots and lettuce and cook together gently for 5 minutes. Add the peas, salt, sugar and thyme. Cover the pan tightly and simmer for 10 minutes.

Note If the peas are rather tough, longer cooking may be needed. Thrifty French housewives often use the hearts of two lettuces for a salad and the outer leaves for this recipe. Other sweet herbs may be substituted for thyme.

Fraises au fromage blanc (page 70)

Crêpes Suzette au Curaçao (page 70)

EPINARDS A L'AIL
Garlic spinach

IMPERIAL/METRIC	AMERICAN
2 oz./50 g. butter	$\frac{1}{4}$ cup butter
2 cloves garlic	2 cloves garlic
2 teaspoons lemon juice	2 teaspoons lemon juice
2 lb./900 g. spinach	2 lb. spinach
$\frac{1}{4}$ pint/1$\frac{1}{2}$ dl. cream	$\frac{2}{3}$ cup cream
salt and pepper	salt and pepper

Pound together the butter, crushed garlic and lemon juice. Heat the mixture in a deep saucepan. Wash the spinach carefully and remove any coarse stems. Shake dry and add to the melted garlic butter. Turn constantly to ensure an even coating of butter. Cook gently for 10 minutes. Remove the spinach from the pan and chop finely. Stir in the cream and seasoning. Heat through gently in a clean saucepan.

CHAMPIGNONS A LA CREME
Mushroom caps in cream

IMPERIAL/METRIC	AMERICAN
1 lb./450 g. button mushrooms	4 cups button mushrooms
3 oz./75 g. butter	6 tablespoons butter
2 cloves garlic, crushed	2 cloves garlic, crushed
1 tablespoon lemon juice	1 tablespoon lemon juice
salt and freshly ground white pepper	salt and freshly ground white pepper
4 tablespoons cream	$\frac{1}{3}$ cup heavy cream
2 teaspoons chopped parsley	2 teaspoons chopped parsley

Wipe the mushrooms and remove the stems. Melt the butter in a sauté pan. Add the mushrooms, garlic, lemon juice and seasoning. Simmer, uncovered, for 10 minutes. Stir in the cream and let it bubble gently. Add the parsley and serve when the cream has thickened slightly.

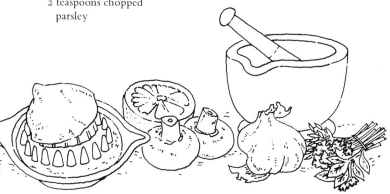

POTEE DE CHOU
Braised cabbage

IMPERIAL/METRIC	AMERICAN
$\frac{1}{2}$ oz./15 g. butter	1 tablespoon butter
1 tablespoon oil	1 tablespoon oil
1 onion, chopped	1 onion, chopped
2 carrots, chopped	2 carrots, chopped
1 lb./450 g. potatoes, diced	1 lb. potatoes, diced
$\frac{1}{4}$ pint/1$\frac{1}{2}$ dl. chicken stock	$\frac{2}{3}$ cup chicken bouillon
2 lb./900 g. white cabbage, shredded	2 lb. white cabbage, shredded
salt and pepper	salt and pepper
1 sprig thyme, chopped	1 sprig thyme, chopped

Heat the butter and oil in a heavy saucepan and brown the onion and carrots. Add the potatoes and just cover with the chicken stock. Place the shredded cabbage on top and cover closely. Simmer for 1 hour. Remove from the heat, add the salt, pepper and thyme and stir well. Cover again and continue cooking gently for another hour. Serve with plain boiled beef.

CELERI A LA FERMIERE
Farmhouse celery

IMPERIAL/METRIC	AMERICAN
1 head celery	1 bunch celery
4 oz./100 g. mushrooms	1 cup mushrooms
1 tablespoon tomato purée	1 tablespoon tomato paste
bouquet garni	bouquet garni
2 cloves garlic, chopped	2 cloves garlic, chopped
1 piece lemon peel, blanched	1 piece lemon peel, blanched
2 tablespoons oil	3 tablespoons oil
salt and freshly ground white pepper	salt and freshly ground white pepper

Wash the celery and cut into 2-inch (5-cm.) lengths. Wipe over and roughly chop the mushrooms. Dilute the tomatoe purée with 1 tablespoon cold water. Place the celery and mushrooms in an ovenproof casserole and stir in the tomato purée. Add the bouquet garni, garlic and lemon peel. Cover tightly, first with greaseproof paper and then the lid. Cook in a moderate oven (325°F., 170°C., Gas Mark 3) for 1½ hours. Heat the oil and stir with the salt and pepper into the cooked vegetables just before serving.

COURGETTES FARCIES
Baked stuffed courgettes

IMPERIAL/METRIC	AMERICAN
1 sprig thyme, chopped	1 sprig thyme, chopped
1 tablespoon chopped parsley	1 tablespoon chopped parsley
4 large tomatoes	4 large tomatoes
1 oz./25 g. butter	2 tablespoons butter
1 tablespoon oil	1 tablespoon oil
1 medium-sized onion, chopped	1 medium-sized onion, chopped
2 cloves garlic, crushed	2 cloves garlic, crushed
salt and freshly ground black pepper	salt and freshly ground black pepper
4 medium-sized courgettes	4 medium-sized zucchini
½ oz./15 g. Parmesan cheese, grated	2 tablespoons grated Parmesan cheese
2 tablespoons fresh breadcrumbs	3 tablespoons fresh bread crumbs

Make sure the herbs are chopped very finely. Skin, deseed and chop the tomatoes. Heat half the butter and the oil together in a frying pan and cook the onion and garlic until soft. Add the tomatoes and seasonings. Remove the tops and tails from the courgettes and cut them in half lengthwise. Scoop out the seed pulp and discard it. Blanch the courgettes in boiling salted water for 2 minutes. Drain and pat dry with kitchen paper. Stuff each courgette with the onion mixture and top with grated cheese and breadcrumbs. Place in a casserole, dot with remaining butter and cook in a moderate oven (350°F., 180°C., Gas Mark 4) for 15 minutes. Brown under a hot grill just before serving.

ASPERGES AVEC SAUCE MORNAY
Asparagus in cheese sauce

IMPERIAL/METRIC	AMERICAN
1 lb./450 g. asparagus, trimmed	1 lb. asparagus, trimmed
1 oz./25 g. butter	2 tablespoons butter
2 oz./50 g. Gruyère cheese, grated	½ cup grated Gruyère cheese
½ pint/3 dl. béchamel sauce (see page 66)	1¼ cups béchamel sauce (see page 66)
½ oz./15 g. Parmesan cheese, grated	2 tablespoons grated Parmesan cheese
2 tablespoons oil	3 tablespoons oil
salt and freshly ground white pepper	salt and freshly ground white pepper

Clean the asparagus and remove all woody parts; cut each spear in two. Place in a well buttered shallow ovenproof dish. Spread the rest of the butter over the asparagus, cover closely to prevent any loss of moisture and cook in a moderately hot oven (375°F., 190°C., Gas Mark 5) for 25 minutes, until the asparagus is tender. Meanwhile, stir the Gruyère into the hot béchamel sauce until melted, then remove from the heat. Strain in any juices from the casserole and stir well. Mask the asparagus with the sauce, sprinkle with the Parmesan and return to the oven, increasing the heat to hot (425°F., 220°C., Gas Mark 7), for 10 minutes.

Tarte au fromage blanc (page 73)

Brioche de fête au sabayon (page 74)

SALADS

SALADE DE SAISON
Green salad

Any green salad may be offered according to what is available from the following – lettuce, corn salad, endive, chicory, watercress, celery, celeriac, chervil, even dandelion leaves. Sometimes fresh herbs (chives, parsley, tarragon, etc.) are added, though not those with woody stems such as rosemary. The service of the salad is important; vinaigrette dressing is placed in the bowl and the salad lightly laid on top. When it is about to be served (and not a moment before) the hostess turns the salad delicately until each leaf is coated with a film of dressing and it is eaten at once. It is never dressed in advance or it goes limp.

The leaves are torn, not cut. Vegetables which require *cutting* such as cucumber, green or red peppers and tomatoes are only included in the south. Herbs, of course, are chopped. Great care is taken to wash the salad and dry it completely without bruising the leaves. Housewives are often to be seen around lunchtime popping outside the back door to whirl a wire salad shaker free of moisture.

Salade aux chapons Rub stale bread with cut garlic, dice and fry in olive oil, or merely sprinkle the uncooked dice with oil. Toss with the dressing into a green salad. Do not combine in advance or the *chapons* become soft.

SAUCE VINAIGRETTE
French dressing

IMPERIAL/METRIC	AMERICAN
½ teaspoon salt	½ teaspoon salt
¼ teaspoon pepper	¼ teaspoon pepper
½ teaspoon mild mustard	½ teaspoon mild mustard
1 tablespoon finely chopped shallot	1 tablespoon finely chopped shallot
1 tablespoon finely chopped fresh herbs	1 tablespoon finely chopped fresh herbs
2 tablespoons wine vinegar	3 tablespoons wine vinegar
4 tablespoons olive or corn oil	⅓ cup olive or corn oil

Mix the seasonings, shallot and herbs with the vinegar. (In some recipes a little sugar is added, but although I prefer this personally it is not typical.) Then beat in the oil. Or at this stage pour the vinegar mixture into a screwtop bottle, add the oil, stopper and shake to emulsify. The herbs may be a selection of parsley, thyme, marjoram, chervil or tarragon. For special occasions, beat in the yolk of a softly boiled egg, to give a more creamy consistency. For short-term storage a peeled clove of garlic can be added to a bottle of vinaigrette sauce. In a cold place it keeps for up to a week at least.

SALADE MONEGASQUE
Monaco salad

IMPERIAL/METRIC	AMERICAN
2 hard-boiled eggs	2 hard-boiled eggs
4 tomatoes	4 tomatoes
4 small white onions	4 small white onions
1 slice ham	1 slice ham
1 red pepper	1 red sweet pepper
1 green pepper	1 green sweet pepper
1 can anchovy fillets	1 can anchovy fillets
4 tablespoons sauce vinaigrette (see preceding recipe)	$\frac{1}{3}$ cup sauce vinaigrette (see preceding recipe)
1 7-oz./198-g. can tuna, drained	1 7-oz. can tuna, drained
4 small gherkins	4 small dill-pickled cucumbers
12 black olives	12 ripe olives
8 green olives	8 green olives

Quarter the eggs and tomatoes, chop the onion and ham, deseed and slice the peppers. Drain the anchovy fillets and add the oil to the vinaigrette. Put the flaked tuna in the bottom of a salad dish, combine the rest of the ingredients and lay on top. Serve with the dressing separately.

Illustrated on page 64

SALADE DE POISSON AU CONCOMBRE
Fish and cucumber salad

IMPERIAL/METRIC	AMERICAN
1 1- to 1$\frac{1}{2}$-lb./450- to 675-g. codling	1 1- to 1$\frac{1}{2}$-lb. young cod
salt and freshly ground black pepper	salt and freshly ground black pepper
1 sprig fennel	1 sprig fennel
1 pat butter	1 pat butter
4 small potatoes	4 small potatoes
4-inch/10-cm. length cucumber, peeled	4-inch length cucumber, peeled
4 tablespoons cream	$\frac{1}{3}$ cup cream
2 teaspoons lemon juice	2 teaspoons lemon juice
1 tablespoon chopped parsley	1 tablespoon chopped parsley

Cook the fish with salt, pepper, a sprig of fennel and the butter *en papillote* (in a foil or greaseproof paper parcel, see page 42). Meanwhile, boil the potatoes in their skins until just tender. Cool slightly and remove the skins. Cut into large dice and pour over the liquid from the fish parcel while the potatoes are still warm enough to absorb it. Roughly flake the fish and add to the potatoes. Chill. Grate or liquidise the cucumber. Half whip the cream, stir in the lemon juice, cucumber, parsley and salt and pepper to taste. Fold the fish mixture into this cream sauce and serve chilled in a shallow glass dish.

TOMATES EN SALADE A LA CREME
Tomato salad with cream

IMPERIAL/METRIC	AMERICAN
1 lb./450 g. medium-sized tomatoes	1 lb. medium-sized tomatoes
2 teaspoons finely chopped tarragon	2 teaspoons finely chopped tarragon
generous $\frac{1}{4}$ pint/1$\frac{1}{2}$ dl. cream	$\frac{3}{4}$ cup heavy cream
salt and freshly ground white pepper	salt and freshly ground white pepper

Peel the tomatoes and stand them upright in a shallow dish. Stir the tarragon into the cream. Add salt and pepper and mix well. Keep cold. Pour the cream over the tomatoes immediately before serving.

Salade monégasque (page 63)

DÉJEUNER SUR L'HERBE

These dishes, shown in colour on the back cover, help to make up a typical French picnic spread.

CONFIT DE PORC
Jellied pork

IMPERIAL/METRIC	AMERICAN
2 lb./900 g. boned loin of pork	2 lb. boned pork loin
salt and freshly ground white pepper	salt and freshly ground white pepper
8-oz./225-g. slice pork fat, cut thinly	½-lb. slice fat back, cut thinly

Sprinkle the joint generously with salt and pepper. Put a small piece of the fat in the bottom of a large fruit juice can (about 2 lb. 3-oz., 1-kg. size), wrap the joint of pork in the rest of the fat and put it into the can which it should almost fill. Cover the top of the can with a double thickness of foil and tie tightly with string. Place in a water bath or deep saucepan and simmer for 3 hours. Remove and cool, when the juices will have set like a jelly. To remove the pork from the can, open the other end of the can, run hot water over the outside, loosen the jelly with a palette knife and push out onto a serving plate. Serve cold.

PAIN AU NOIX
Nut bread

IMPERIAL/METRIC	AMERICAN
1 oz./25 g. baker's yeast	1 cake compressed yeast
1 pint/5½ dl. water	2½ cups water
2¼ lb./1 kg. strong plain flour	9 cups bread flour
¾ oz./20 g. salt	1 tablespoon salt
6 oz./175 g. nuts, crushed	1½ cups crushed nuts

Dissolve the yeast in warm water. Knead the liquid into the flour sieved with the salt. Allow to rise for 2 hours. Knock back, work in the crushed nuts. Knead again thoroughly. Make the paste into two balls, allow to rise again, and bake the loaves in a very hot oven (475°F., 240°C., Gas Mark 9) for 20 minutes. Serve with butter and an assortment of *charcuterie*, or cream cheese.

Note The nuts are usually walnuts, but any assortment of nuts will do.

SAUCES AND DRESSINGS

SAUCES
Sauces

The two most useful savoury sauces are Béchamel (white roux) and Espagnole (brown roux). A roux is a blend of butter and flour, which thickens the sauce and imparts a smooth, creamy texture. If the flour is fully absorbed by the butter, the liquid can be added all at once and whisked in (not stirred) though it is easier to produce a smooth result if the liquid is warm.

White roux Melt $2\frac{1}{2}$ oz. (60 g., $\frac{1}{3}$ cup) butter, stir in 2 oz. (50 g., $\frac{1}{2}$ cup) flour and cook, stirring constantly, for 2 minutes.

Brown roux Continue cooking the white roux until mixture is golden brown.

BÉCHAMEL SAUCE

Slowly warm 1 pint ($5\frac{1}{2}$ dl., $2\frac{1}{2}$ cups) milk with a chopped shallot or small onion, a sliced carrot, a chopped stalk of celery, and some spices – a few peppercorns, a bay leaf and a blade of mace. When the milk comes to the boil, withdraw the pan from heat, cover and allow to stand for 20 minutes to infuse. Make a white roux, whisk in the strained milk and add sufficient salt to taste. Bring to the boil and whisk (or stir) over moderate heat for 4–5 minutes. Makes 1 pint sauce.

Sauce aurore Add $\frac{1}{2}$ pint (3 dl., $1\frac{1}{4}$ cups) sieved tomato purée (or 3 tablespoons tomato paste with 1 teaspoon sugar), $\frac{1}{2}$ teaspoon salt and $\frac{1}{4}$ teaspoon pepper to $\frac{1}{2}$ pint (3 dl., $1\frac{1}{4}$ cups) béchamel sauce. Serve with chicken and fish.

ESPAGNOLE SAUCE

Melt 2 oz. (50g., $\frac{1}{4}$ cup) meat dripping or butter, add 2 oz. (50 g., $\frac{1}{4}$ cup) diced fat bacon and 2 oz. (50 g., $\frac{1}{2}$ cup) chopped carrot and onion. Fry until soft but not brown. Stir in 2 oz. (50 g., $\frac{1}{2}$ cup) flour and cook slowly until it turns a rich brown. Add 1 pint ($5\frac{1}{2}$ dl., $2\frac{1}{2}$ cups) beef stock, 2 tablespoons tomato purée, salt, sugar and pepper to taste and whisk until boiling. Simmer, covered, for about 30 minutes. Strain, add 1 tablespoon sherry and if sauce is too thick, a little more stock. Makes 1 pint sauce.

Sauce Madère Stir 2 tablespoons Madeira into $\frac{1}{2}$ pint (3 dl., $1\frac{1}{4}$ cups) Espagnole sauce and reheat without boiling. Serve with meat.

Fond blanc White meat or chicken stock, made by simmering chicken or veal bones with chopped root vegetables and seasoning for several hours. Cool, strain and when cold remove fat.

Fond brun Beef stock, made by simmering beef bones and trimmings as for *fond blanc*.

HOLLANDAISE SAUCE

Heat 2 tablespoons lemon juice and 1 tablespoon water together in a bowl over simmering water. Whisk in 2 egg yolks and a small nut of butter. When the sauce is thick, remove from the heat and gradually whisk in more butter, up to the weight of the 2 whole eggs. Serve with fish and green vegetables.

BEURRE A L'AIL
Garlic butter

IMPERIAL/METRIC	AMERICAN
4 shallots or 8 spring onions	4 shallots or 8 scallions
3 cloves garlic	3 cloves garlic
2 tablespoons finely chopped parsley	3 tablespoons finely chopped parsley
pinch pepper	pinch pepper
pinch mixed spice	pinch mixed spice
8 oz./225 g. salted butter	1 cup salted butter

Very finely chop the shallots (or white part of the spring onions) and the garlic. Mix with the parsley and seasonings. Soften the butter with a fork and beat in the other ingredients with a wooden spoon. Put in a closed container and chill for about an hour before serving.

Note This butter is served with snails, cooked vegetables and grilled steaks.

MAYONNAISE
Mayonnaise

IMPERIAL/METRIC	AMERICAN
2 egg yolks or 1 whole egg and 1 egg yolk	2 egg yolks or 1 whole egg and 1 egg yolk
1 teaspoon Dijon mustard	1 teaspoon Dijon mustard
$\frac{1}{4}$ teaspoon salt	$\frac{1}{4}$ teaspoon salt
$\frac{1}{4}$ teaspoon pepper	$\frac{1}{4}$ teaspoon pepper
$\frac{1}{2}$ pint/3 dl. olive oil	$1\frac{1}{4}$ cups olive oil
1 tablespoon wine vinegar	1 tablespoon wine vinegar

Make sure that all ingredients are at room temperature. Put the eggs and seasonings into a bowl. Whisk to a smooth consistency and begin adding the oil, at first a few drops at a time. Whisk steadily until nearly all the oil has been added. When the mayonnaise is fairly stiff, beat in the vinegar and then add the rest of the oil. Taste and adjust seasoning if necessary. Serve with cold dishes. These quantities give $\frac{1}{2}$ pint (3 dl., $1\frac{1}{4}$ cups).

Variations

MAYONNAISE MOUSSELINE
Beat one egg white until stiff then fold into $\frac{1}{2}$ pint mayonnaise. Serve with white fish.

SAUCE TARTARE
Add 1 teaspoon each chopped capers, gherkins, fresh mixed herbs and grated onion to $\frac{1}{2}$ pint mayonnaise.

SAUCE REMOULADE
Add 1 tablespoon Dijon mustard and 1 tablespoon very finely chopped shallot or white part of spring onion, to $\frac{1}{2}$ pint mayonnaise.

SAUCE AIOLI
Pound 2 crushed garlic cloves to a paste before putting in the egg yolks, then make mayonnaise in the usual way.

LA TAPENADE
Black olive pâté

IMPERIAL/METRIC	AMERICAN
4 anchovy fillets	4 anchovy fillets
12 oz./350 g. black olives	2 cups ripe olives
¼ teaspoon ground thyme	¼ teaspoon ground thyme
¼ teaspoon ground marjoram	¼ teaspoon ground marjoram
¼ teaspoon ground bay leaves	¼ teaspoon ground bay leaves
1 teaspoon Dijon mustard	1 teaspoon Dijon mustard
2 teaspoons wine vinegar	2 teaspoons wine vinegar
1 teaspoon brandy	1 teaspoon brandy
6 tablespoons olive oil	½ cup olive oil

Soak the anchovy fillets to remove excess salt, stone the olives, and if necessary pound the seasonings to a powder with a pestle and mortar. Mix all the ingredients together well, adding the oil last, a few drops at a time, and beat thoroughly. Pass through a sieve or liquidise in an electric blender. Turn into a wide-necked jar, cover with a circle of waxed paper or foil. Allow to mature for a few days and use as a spread on *tartines* or *croûtes* to float on soup, etc. It keeps for weeks in a cool place.

Note Plain boiled vegetables, which are somewhat unflatteringly described as *à l'anglaise* in France, are often topped with a spoonful of *la tapénade* in the Midi.

CREME ST. HONORE
Cream filling for cakes

IMPERIAL/METRIC	AMERICAN
1 oz./25 g. flour	¼ cup flour
4 oz./100 g. sugar	½ cup sugar
few drops vanilla essence	few drops vanilla extract
4 eggs	4 eggs
1 pint/5½ dl. milk	2½ cups milk

Mix the flour, sugar, vanilla, 1 whole egg and the 3 yolks together. Bring the milk to the boil and whisk into the mixture gradually. Whisk over a low heat for several minutes until thick and smooth. Remove from the heat. Beat the 3 egg whites and fold in while the cream is still warm. Cool and use to fill choux puffs (see page 75) or spread under fruit in a flan.

DESSERTS HOT AND COLD

SOUFFLE AU LIQUEUR
Soufflé with liqueur

IMPERIAL/METRIC	AMERICAN
finely grated zest of	finely grated zest of
1 orange	1 orange
2½ oz./60 g. sugar	⅓ cup sugar
scant ½ pint/2½ dl. milk	1 cup milk
1 oz./25 g. flour	¼ cup flour
¾ oz./20 g. butter	1½ tablespoons butter
5 eggs, separated	5 eggs, separated
4 tablespoons Grand Marnier or Cointreau	⅓ cup Grand Marnier or Cointreau

Place the orange zest and sugar in a saucepan with most of the milk, reserving 3 tablespoons to blend with the flour. Heat to just below boiling point. Remove the pan from the heat and allow the milk to infuse for 10 minutes. Whisk together the flour and reserved milk, gradually whisk in the flavoured milk, return to the pan and bring to the boil. Boil for 2 minutes, whisking continuously until the mixture forms a smooth paste, remove from heat and beat in the butter, then the egg yolks one at a time. Add the liqueur with the last egg yolk. Fold in the stiffly beaten egg whites and pour into a buttered 2-pint (1-litre, 5-cup) soufflé dish. Cook in the centre of a moderate oven (350°F., 180°C., Gas Mark 4) for about 30 minutes, or until well risen and golden brown. Serve immediately.

Note This soufflé is a favourite choice with my relatives for children's birthdays and Saints' days. On such occasions glacé cherries soaked overnight in the same liqueur are folded into the mixture before adding the egg whites.

COEUR A LA CREME
Cream hearts to serve with fruit

IMPERIAL/METRIC	AMERICAN
8 oz./225 g. cottage cheese	1 cup cottage cheese
½ pint/3 dl. cream, whipped	1¼ cups cream, whipped
1 tablespoon icing sugar	1 tablespoon confectioners' sugar

Sieve the cottage cheese twice. Stir in the cream and sieved icing sugar. In France it is set in heart-shaped moulds with a perforated base to allow the whey to drip through but there is very little whey with our cottage cheese, so it may be formed into round flat cakes and drained on soft kitchen paper.

FRAISES AU FROMAGE BLANC
Strawberries with cheese cream

IMPERIAL/METRIC	AMERICAN
2 lb./900 g. sweetened strawberries	2 lb. sweetened strawberries
½ pint/3 dl. creamy milk	1¼ cups creamy milk
1 tablespoon castor sugar	1 tablespoon sugar
2 Petit-suisse cheeses	2 Petit-suisse or other unsalted cream cheese

Hull and wash the strawberries and sweeten with sugar if necessary. Beat the milk and castor sugar into the cheese until they have the consistency of half-whipped double cream. Sweeten further if liked. Serve mixed with the strawberries.

Illustrated on page 56

Note This is a favourite sweet with children. The cheese is sometimes eaten without fruit and sprinkled with plenty of sugar, or with jam stirred into it.

CREPES SUZETTE AU CURACAO
Sweet pancakes in tangerine sauce

IMPERIAL/METRIC	AMERICAN
Pancakes	
4 oz./100 g. plain flour	1 cup all-purpose flour
pinch salt	pinch salt
1 egg and 1 egg yolk	1 egg and 1 egg yolk
1 tablespoon oil	1 tablespoon oil
½ pint/2½ dl. milk and tangerine juice	1¼ cups milk and tangerine juice
1 tablespoon Curaçao	1 tablespoon Curaçao
oil or butter for frying	oil or butter for frying
Filling	
2 oz./50 g. unsalted butter	¼ cup sweet butter
2 oz./50 g. castor sugar	¼ cup sugar
2 tablespoons tangerine juice	3 tablespoons tangerine juice
grated zest of 1 tangerine	grated zest of 1 tangerine
1 tablespoon Curaçao	1 tablespoon Curaçao

Sieve the flour and salt into a bowl. Make a well in the centre and tip in the egg and egg yolk. Add the oil and 2 tablespoons milk. Begin to beat in the flour, adding more milk, a few tablespoons of tangerine juice and then the rest of the milk to make a smooth runny cream. Leave to stand for 1 hour. Beat in the Curaçao. Fry eight thin pancakes, in a small pan lightly oiled or buttered, until golden brown on both sides. Keep hot until all are cooked.

To make the filling, cream the butter and sugar and beat in the tangerine juice, zest and Curaçao. Spread each pancake with filling and fold in four. Arrange overlapping in a pan over a chafing dish, pour any remaining juice from the tangerines over and serve very hot.

Illustrated on page 57

Note In France the dish is not often flambéed, but 2 tablespoons brandy can be warmed, ignited, and poured over the pancakes just before serving. Oranges are substituted when tangerines are not available.

CLAFOUTI
Cherry batter pudding

IMPERIAL/METRIC	AMERICAN
6 eggs	6 eggs
3 oz./75 g. sugar	6 tablespoons sugar
pinch salt	pinch salt
3½ oz./90 g. flour	⅞ cup flour
½ pint/2½ dl. milk	1¼ cups milk
2 lb./900 g. black cherries	2 lb. Bing cherries
2 tablespoons Kirsch	3 tablespoons Kirsch
icing sugar, to sprinkle	confectioners' sugar, to sprinkle

Beat the eggs, sugar, salt and flour together. Add a little milk. Beat again and add the rest of the milk, beating all the time. The batter should be as runny as a crêpe batter. Remove the stalks and stones from the cherries. (Tante Joséphine uses the rounded end of a strong, old fashioned hairpin to hook out the stones.) Put the cherries into a shallow ovenproof dish and pour over the Kirsch. Cover with the batter and cook in a moderately hot oven (400°F., 200°C., Gas Mark 6) for 35 minutes. Sprinkle with icing sugar through a sieve. Serve cold.

GATEAU AU RIZ
Caramel rice pudding

IMPERIAL/METRIC	AMERICAN
6 oz./175 g. round-grain rice	scant cup short-grain rice
2 pints/generous litre milk	5 cups milk
pinch salt	pinch salt
3 oz./75 g. sugar	6 tablespoons sugar
few drops vanilla essence	few drops vanilla extract
2 eggs	2 eggs
4 oz./100 g. raisins	¾ cup raisins
Caramel	
3 oz./75 g. sugar	6 tablespoons sugar

Cook the rice in the milk with the salt, sugar and vanilla until tender. Remove from heat, stir in the egg yolks and raisins and fold in the stiffly beaten egg whites. Melt the sugar for the caramel in a heavy pan until it becomes a rich golden brown. Pour quickly into a 2-pint (1-litre, 5-cup) mould, turning to coat all sides evenly. Pour in the rice mixture and put into centre of a hot oven (425°F., 220°C., Gas Mark 7) for 10 minutes. Allow to cool, chill and turn out. Serve with a compote of fruit or with whipped cream.

Note For special occasions, add powdered saffron and chopped glacé cherries to the rice mixture, with 2 tablespoons rum.

CREMES AU CHOCOLAT
Chocolate pots

IMPERIAL/METRIC	AMERICAN
4 oz./100 g. dark chocolate	⅔ cup semisweet chocolate pieces
4 eggs, separated	4 eggs, separated
3 tablespoons cream	¼ cup heavy cream
2½ oz./60 g. icing sugar	⅔ cup confectioners' sugar
1 tablespoon brandy	1 tablespoon brandy
1 teaspoon finely grated orange zest	1 teaspoon finely grated orange zest
4 strips orange peel, blanched	4 strips orange peel, blanched

Melt the chocolate in a basin over hot water. Remove from the heat and beat in the egg yolks, cream, icing sugar, brandy and orange zest. Fold in the stiffly beaten egg whites until well blended and pour into individual cocotte dishes. Chill and serve topped with a curl of orange peel.

LES OEUFS A LA NEIGE AU CITRON
Snow eggs

IMPERIAL/METRIC	AMERICAN
5 eggs, separated	5 eggs, separated
finely grated zest of ½ lemon	finely grated zest of ½ lemon
1 pint/5½ dl. milk	2½ cups milk
strip lemon peel	strip lemon peel
8 oz./225 g. castor sugar	1 cup sugar

Whisk the egg whites until they form firm peaks. Fold in the lemon zest. Beat the egg yolks together and add 2 tablespoons cold milk. Bring the rest of the milk to the boil, add the lemon peel and stir in the sugar. Drop teaspoons of the egg whites into the hot milk and poach them gently for 2 minutes. Turn them once with a slotted draining spoon. Drain on kitchen paper and place in a shallow dish. Cool the milk and stir in the egg yolks. Heat the mixture gently over simmering water, stirring continuously. The mixture will gradually thicken but must not boil. Remove the lemon peel. Cool the custard and pour round the snow balls. Serve chilled.

Note This is a very sweet custard and the sugar may be reduced to 6 oz. (175 g., ¾ cup) if preferred.

PATISSERIE AND CONFITURES

GALETTE A LA FERMIERE
Farmhouse cake

IMPERIAL/METRIC	AMERICAN
4 oz./100 g. flour	1 cup all-purpose flour
4 oz./100 g. castor sugar	½ cup sugar
4 oz./100 g. clotted cream	½ cup clotted cream
few drops vanilla essence	few drops vanilla essence
1 egg yolk	1 egg yolk

Sieve the flour into a bowl, mix in the sugar, cream and flavouring by hand, knead lightly and press into a shallow round flan tin. Brush with egg yolk and bake in a moderate oven (350°F., 180°C., Gas Mark 4) for 35–40 minutes. Cool and serve cut into wedges.

Note The more usual galette bretonne is made with 3 oz. (75 g., 6 tablespoons) unsalted butter and 2 egg yolks instead of the 'boiled cream' as clotted cream is described in France. These flat cakes take the place of sweet biscuits in most French households.

CAKE DES DEBUTANTES
Débutante's cake

IMPERIAL/METRIC	AMERICAN
1 lb./450 g. self-raising flour	4 cups all-purpose flour sifted with 4 teaspoons baking powder
5 eggs	5 eggs
10 oz./275 g. sugar	1⅓ cups sugar
1 large lemon	1 large lemon
pinch salt	pinch salt
6 fl. oz./175 ml. corn oil	¾ cup corn oil
½ pint/275 ml. milk	1¼ cups milk

Sieve the flour into a mixing bowl. Make a hollow in the centre. In another bowl, beat the eggs with the sugar, grated zest of the lemon and the salt. Beat in the oil and milk, adding a little of each alternately. Pour the mixture into the flour, drawing it in gradually, then beat until smooth. Pour into two greased and lined 9- by 5-inch (23- by 13-cm.) loaf tins and bake in a moderate oven (350°F., 180°C., Gas Mark 4) for 50 minutes. If necessary, cover the top of the cakes with greaseproof paper or foil after 25 minutes to prevent overbrowning. Test with a fine skewer, cool for a few minutes in the tin and turn out. This cake stays moist for a week.

Note Most girls learn how to make this cake before attempting to make pastry.

TARTE AU FROMAGE BLANC
Sweet cheese tart

IMPERIAL/METRIC	AMERICAN
Pâte brisée	
2 tablespoons water	3 tablespoons water
4 oz./100 g. butter, diced	½ cup butter, diced
1 egg	1 egg
8 oz./225 g. plain flour	2 cups all-purpose flour
pinch salt	pinch salt
Filling	
12 oz./350 g. cream cheese	1½ cups cream cheese
8 oz./225 g. castor sugar	1 cup sugar
¼ pint/1½ dl. cream	⅔ cup cream
4 eggs	4 eggs
2 oz./50 g. seedless raisins	⅓ cup seedless raisins
4 oz./100 g. mixed candied fruits	¾ cup mixed candied fruits

Illustrated on page 60

To make the *pâte brisée*, mix together the water, diced butter and egg. Sieve the flour and salt together, make a well in the centre and pour in the mixture. Work together lightly with the fingertips, gradually drawing in the flour. Knead lightly, form into a ball, cover and chill for 30 minutes. Roll out and use to line a 10-inch (25-cm.) flan ring. Bake blind in a moderately hot oven (375°F., 190°C., Gas Mark 5) for 10 minutes. Meanwhile, make the filling. Beat together the cream cheese, sugar, cream and eggs. Fold in the raisins and finely chopped candied fruits. Turn into the pastry case. Bake in a moderately hot oven (375°F., 190°C., Gas Mark 5) for 30 minutes, then reduce the temperature to cool (300°F., 150°C., Gas Mark 2) and cook for a further 20 minutes until the filling is set and browned. Serve hot or cold.

Note This quantity serves eight. You could bake it in two 6-inch (15-cm.) flans if you roll the pastry out very thinly.

MADELEINES
Madeleines

IMPERIAL/METRIC	AMERICAN
4 eggs	4 eggs
6 oz./175 g. castor sugar	¾ cup sugar
8 oz./225 g. self-raising flour	2 cups all-purpose flour sifted with 2 teaspoons baking powder
1 lemon	1 lemon
3½ oz./90 g. butter	7 tablespoons butter

Beat the eggs and sugar together until pale and fluffy. Gradually beat in the sieved flour and the grated zest of the lemon and finally fold in the melted butter. Prepare a Madeleine tin by greasing lightly with butter, then sieve in some flour and tip out the surplus. Half fill the shapes with the mixture and allow to stand for 15 minutes. Bake in the centre of a very hot oven (475°F., 240°C., Gas Mark 9) for 10 minutes or until golden brown. Cool and serve fresh or keep in a tin for several days. If you have to use the same tin twice, cool before refilling. Makes 24.

SABLES DE TROUVILLE
Sand biscuits

IMPERIAL/METRIC	AMERICAN
1 egg	1 egg
4 oz./100 g. sugar	½ cup sugar
pinch salt	pinch salt
8 oz./225 g. plain flour	2 cups all-purpose flour
4 oz./100 g. butter	½ cup butter
1 teaspoon vanilla essence	1 teaspoon vanilla extract
1 teaspoon grated lemon zest	1 teaspoon grated lemon zest

Beat together the egg, sugar and salt until pale and foamy. Stir in the flour and mix well (the mixture will be crumbly at this stage). Turn out on a cold surface and add the softened butter and flavouring, first mixing with a fork and then kneading by hand. Shape into a roll and chill in the refrigerator for 30 minutes. Cut thin slices from the roll, about ⅛ inch (3 mm.) thick. Place on an ungreased baking sheet and bake in the centre of a moderate oven (350°F., 180°C., Gas Mark 4) for 15 minutes. Cool on a wire rack. Serve plain, or sprinkled with castor sugar. Store in a tin to keep crisp. Makes 30 *sablés*.

BRIOCHE
Brioche

IMPERIAL/METRIC	AMERICAN
½ oz./15 g. fresh or 2 teaspoons dried yeast	½ cake compressed or 2 teaspoons active dry yeast
2 tablespoons warm milk	3 tablespoons warm milk
8 oz./225 g. plain flour	2 cups all-purpose flour
3 eggs	3 eggs
4 oz./100 g. butter, softened	½ cup softened butter
pinch salt	pinch salt
1 oz./25 g. sugar	2 tablespoons sugar

Glaze

1 tablespoon sugar dissolved in 2 tablespoons water	1 tablespoon sugar dissolved in 2 tablespoons water

Mix the yeast with the warm milk and 2 tablespoons of the flour. Leave to stand in a floured bowl for 6 hours. This is the leaven. When it has doubled in size, mix together the rest of the flour, the eggs, softened butter, and the salt and sugar dissolved in 2 tablespoons warm water. Mix to a firm dough. Work in the leaven, knead and put in a greased bowl, covered with a polythene bag, in a warm place overnight. Next morning, knock back, knead again lightly, reserve one third of the dough and put the remainder into a brioche mould, well buttered. Press a hole in the centre and put the reserved dough, shaped into a ball, on the top. Cook in a moderately hot oven (375°F., 190°C., Gas Mark 5) for 50 minutes. Brush with sugar syrup while the brioche is still warm.

Note Small brioches can be made by a quicker method, but the traditional method, which requires the dough to be begun the day *before* it is cooked, gives a better result.

PAIN PERDU DE JOSETTE
Josette's brioche fritters

Leftover brioche turns this simple nursery dish into a treat. Beat 2 eggs with ¾ pint (4 dl., 2 cups) milk and 4 oz. (100 g., ½ cup) castor sugar. Dip thin slices of stale brioche into the mixture leaving for 30 seconds only, while a nut of butter heats in a frying pan. Brown the slices on both sides, adding fresh butter as required, and serve the slices sprinkled with vanilla sugar or cinnamon and sugar.

BRIOCHE DE FETE AU SABAYON
Brioche with sabayon sauce

IMPERIAL/METRIC	AMERICAN
1 large brioche (see above)	1 large brioche (see above)

Sauce

6 egg yolks	6 egg yolks
6 oz./175 g. castor sugar	¾ cup sugar
½ pint/275 ml. sweet white wine (Sauternes)	1¼ cups sweet white wine (Sauterne)

Beat the egg yolks with the sugar until pale and foamy. Put in a double boiler, add the wine and beat vigorously over a low heat until the sauce thickens. Remove from the heat and continue beating until the sauce cools, pour into a serving bowl and serve cold with the brioche.

Illustrated on page 61

PATE A CHOUX
Choux pastry puffs

IMPERIAL/METRIC	AMERICAN
5 oz./150 g. plain flour	1¼ cups all-purpose flour
¼ teaspoon salt	¼ teaspoon salt
½ pint/3 dl. water	1¼ cups water
4 oz./100 g. butter	½ cup butter
4 eggs	4 eggs

Sieve the flour and salt together. Bring the water and butter to the boil in a saucepan and remove from the heat. Beat in the flour and salt until the mixture forms a ball which leaves the sides of the saucepan clean. Cool to blood heat and beat in the eggs one at a time. Place the mixture in a piping bag and, using a ½-inch (1-cm.) pipe, force ½-inch balls of paste onto wetted baking sheets. Place in the centre of a moderately hot oven (375°F., 190°C., Gas Mark 5) for 20–25 minutes. Cool, and store. Makes about four dozen.

Note For simple occasions, the puffs are merely filled with Crème St. Honoré (see page 68) and sprinkled with icing sugar, or covered with chocolate sauce and served as *profiteroles*.

CROQUEMBOUCHE
Puff pyramid

You will need about eight dozen choux paste puffs (double basic recipe). If the puffs have been stored, spread them out on baking trays and crisp in a moderately hot oven (400°F., 200°C., Gas Mark 6) for 2–3 minutes. Make a hole in the bottom (not the side) of each puff by pressing in the tip of your little finger. Half-whip ½ pint (3 dl., 1¼ cups) double cream with ¼ pint (1½ dl., ⅔ cup) single cream, 2 tablespoons sieved icing sugar and 2 tablespoons brandy, fortified wine or liqueur. Using a large piping bag and any nozzle that fits the diameter of the hole you've made, pipe cream into all the puffs. Do not overfill as cream leaking out makes 'dipping' difficult.

Make up a sugar syrup in two lots, using ¼ pint (1½ dl., ⅔ cup) water and 4 oz. (125 g., ½ cup) sugar each time. Do not stir once the sugar is dissolved, but continue boiling until it is straw coloured (pale golden, not more) then remove the saucepan to a heatproof mat next to the prepared base. This should be a 7- or 8-inch (18- or 20-cm.) cake tin base. Using a dessertspoon with a rather pointed end to the bowl, or a fork, run a line of caramel round the edge, then dip the puffs, holding well clear of the caramel, in at one side and put in place, with the round tops all pointing outwards, to make a circle of about 12 puffs projecting out and concealing the edge of the base. Continue dipping puffs and build up a second circle slightly smaller of about 10 puffs. (This base is the hardest part.) Filling the centre with any badly shaped or coloured puffs, trickle fine filaments of caramel over all the puffs round the outside and, when the sugar starts to cloud, the inside ones where it won't show. As you build up the third and fourth circle, you can mould the shape to keep it even by pressing the pile gently before the sugar is fully set. Try to work so that you use the best puffs and the clearest part of the caramel for the outside and the less good puffs and end of each sugar batch for the centre.

You should have enough to make a rounded pyramid about 15 inches (38 cm.) high. Try making some spun sugar to put in a ball on the top with the last lot of caramel, drizzling from a fork passed to and fro between two wooden rolling pins or even spoon handles to make fine strands which, when cool, you gather up in a ball.

Transfer the finished croquembouche to a serving dish at least 9 inches (23 cm.) in diameter. Whip a further ¼ pint (1½ dl., ⅔ cup) double cream with a little single and use to pipe big rosettes round the base. Spike sugared almonds between the rosettes. Each person should get 3–4 puffs, and a cream rosette and sugared almonds. If the centre puffs are drizzled with caramel at each layer as you build up they have just as nice a crunchy coating as the outside ones.

CONFITURE D'ABRICOTS
Apricot preserve

IMPERIAL/METRIC	AMERICAN
4 lb./1¾ kg. apricots	4 lb. apricots
3 lb./1¼ kg. preserving sugar	3 lb. preserving sugar
½ pint/2½ dl. water	1¼ cups water

Halve the apricots; remove the stones and break them by tapping sharply with a hammer to remove the kernels. Blanch the kernels in boiling water. Put the sugar and water into a preserving pan and heat slowly until the sugar is dissolved. Bring to the boil and allow to boil for 2 minutes, skimming if necessary. Add the apricot halves, bring to the boil again and cook over reduced heat until the jam reaches setting point. Stir in the blanched kernels, allow the jam to cool a little and stir to distribute the fruit evenly, then pot, cover and seal.

GELEE DE RAISINS
Grape jelly

IMPERIAL/METRIC	AMERICAN
8 lb./3½ kg. ripe sweet grapes	8 lb. ripe sweet grapes
4 dessert apples	4 dessert apples
¾ pint/4 dl. water	scant 2 cups water
sugar	sugar
4 tablespoons Kirsch	⅓ cup Kirsch

Crush the grapes, 1 lb. (450 g.) at a time, and keep adding to a large bowl. Stir in the apples, cut in dice without removing skins or cores. Let stand for 2 hours. Transfer to a large preserving pan, add the water and cook gently until the apples are soft. Spread a large square of damp muslin in the large bowl, pour in the cooked fruit, bring up the four corners and tie, so it forms a jelly bag (or use a proper jelly bag). Hang to drip over the bowl, but do not press through or the jelly will be cloudy. When you have extracted all the juice, measure it and allow 1 lb. (450 g.) sugar to each pint (5½ dl., 2½ cups) of juice. Bring to the boil very slowly to let the sugar dissolve, then boil rapidly until setting point is achieved, when it will coat a wooden spoon thickly (about 30–35 minutes). Stir in the Kirsch, pour at once into warm sterilised jars and cover immediately.

Note In wine-growing districts this is more commonly served than any kind of jam, and the colour varies from pale yellow to purple according to the type of grape used.

THE WEALTH OF FRANCE

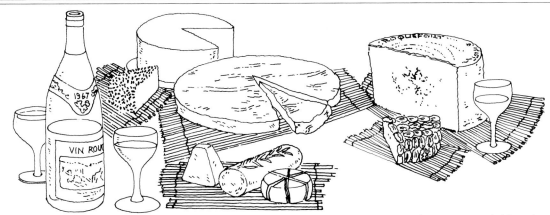

Cheese

Dozens, even hundreds of cheeses, are qualified to be numbered among the cheeses of France. Of these, many are regional and not produced in sufficient quantity to export. But since a very representative selection is exported (and alas imitated), you should be able to present a typical cheese platter, or use in cooking the type a French housewife would herself choose. No main meal in France is quite complete without several cheeses in prime condition and a basket of bread on the table. Cream, soft, semi-hard, hard and even processed cheeses are on the list.

Cream cheese Petit-suisse (which is unsalted and used in sweet dishes for cooking), Demi-sel and various herb and garlic flavoured cream cheeses sold under trade names such as Boursin, are all made from cows' milk. Saint Marcellin is made of a mixture of cows' and goats' milk.

Soft cheese Camembert, most famous of all, comes from Normandy. There are at least three grades of Camembert and the price is governed by the percentage of *matière grasse*, the richest being the most expensive. Like Brie and Coulommiers it has the famous *croûte fleurie*, a delicious crust inside which these delicate cheeses take up to a month to mature. In the same category, but stronger, are Pont l'évêque, Carré de l'Est (which gets its name from the square shape and box), Livarot and Maroilles. Another unusual shape is the oval Caprice des dieux. These cheeses are made in small convenient sizes except for Brie which is made in huge wheels and often cut in wedges, wrapped and packed in export boxes. But I like to buy a wedge cut from the wheel in the market so that I may choose it *bien fait*, ripe for immediate eating. Good shops here sell Brie in the same way.

Semi-hard cheese This includes a vast range of exquisite cheeses, the best known being Saint Paulin, Port-Salut, Reblochon and Tome de Savoie which is enclosed in a lovely brownish purple crust of dried grape pips. Chèvre is merely a generic term for goats' milk cheeses which are crumbly in texture and mild in flavour, but have a certain after-taste which to my mind is very recognisable and reminiscent of the source.

Hard cheese The best known abroad are Munster from Alsace, Emmenthal and Cantal, a cows' milk cheese which is the nearest thing to our Cheddar produced in France.

Blue cheese Roquefort wears the crown of French cheeses. It is strong, even better when very mature, and is made from ewes' milk. My personal favourite is Bleu de Bresse, not so pungent as Roquefort, or possibly Bleu d'Auvergne, even milder still.

Melted or processed cheese These are more popular in France than we suppose, especially processed Gruyère, Fondu aux Noix, which is overcoated in walnut halves.

The right way to store French cheese

Cream cheeses are unfermented and will only keep a few days, even if wrapped in foil or muslin in a cold place such as the refrigerator. Fermented cheeses, that is to say all the other categories, have a longer storage life because they gradually mature. The ripening period to bring soft cheeses to their peak is arrested by refrigeration and they do tend to dehydrate, so take this into account when wrapping and placing in the fridge. By the time you buy an imported soft French cheese it should have only 2–3 days to reach its peak. Cheese which is allowed to become over-mature and is then stored at a low temperature is hard, dark, and slightly ammoniac in flavour. If you buy it this way, return it and ask for your money back. Semi-hard, hard and blue cheeses can be wrapped in damp muslin to keep them moist, but once cut are better closely moulded in foil. Cream cheese is often served chilled, but other cheeses at room temperature.

Wines

Nowhere else in the world is wine so keenly enjoyed and appreciated as in France. The range of French wines is enormous and even on a limited budget it is always possible to effect a perfect marriage between the food on the table and the wine in the glass.

Although the famous Burgundies and Clarets, long our traditional favourites, are soaring in price, there are compensations; a whole new range of French wines, with names as yet unfamiliar, offers new joys to those with a discerning and adventurous palate.

World demand is straining the supply of great wines entitled to bear the *Appellation d'Origine Contrôlée*, which guarantees not only that the wine comes from a specified origin, but is made according to the local practice.

But the V.D.Q.S. label indicates a wine of superior quality – *vins délimités de qualité supérieure*, from the less well known regions. These are simply named wines which fulfil very important conditions regarding the area of production, the vines, methods of growing and wine-making, alcoholic content and maximum yield.

Typical of these are the wines of Languedoc-Corbières and Minervois situated between the Pyrenées and the Mediterranean. Minervois produces largely red wines, which are tender and warm-tasting, and fresh, fruity rosés. Corbières produces strong red wines, rich white wine and elegant rosés. More than half the wines produced in France come from Languedoc.

Other V.D.Q.S. wines becoming increasingly popular are those of the Côtes de Provence which include full-bodied reds, delicate, pale-gold whites and delightful heady rosés.

There are, of course, many *appellation contrôlée* wines still available in considerable quantity at very reasonable prices. These include the splendid red wines of the Côtes du Rhône, including Châteauneuf-du-Pape, Hermitage and, of course, Tavel Rosé. The Loire Valley offers an enormous choice of wines from the fragrant white Sancerre and the spicy white Vouvray to soft red Chinon, Anjou rosé and Muscadet. (Chinon, says Oncle Emile, is perfumed with violets, a charming conviction. He enjoys both the seductive red and the velvety Chinon rosé, quoting the celebrated saying: 'It's a wine for intellectuals.') These contrast perfectly with the elegant white wines of Alsace with its Sylvaner, Riesling and Gewürztraminer – all fruity and beautifully balanced.

Those who are saddened by the mounting price of champagne may wonder who, even in France itself, can afford to serve a *vin mousseux* for an informal afternoon party. The choice would be something less costly. It might be a refreshing Clairette de Die, from the Côtes du Rhône; or a young and lively Blanquette de Limoux from Languedoc. It might not be a sparkling wine at all; the semi-sparkling *pétillant* wines of the Loire are favoured by my family, perhaps because so many of them live in that region. Vouvray, either *mousseux* or *pétillant*, is a frequent choice, but to my mind Anjou and Saumur produce the most delicate and delightful semi-sparkling whites and a gentle rosé much to my taste.

How to marry wine and food

Light red wines and rosé wines All white meats, lamb, veal, turkey, chicken, guinea fowl, pigeon. Grilled cutlets, brochettes, delicate pâtés, fish soup, strongly flavoured hard cheeses and fresh cream cheeses. Green beans, peas, boiled potatoes, dried beans.

Strong red wines with a full body All red meats, duck, chicken in red wine sauce, game such as hare, rabbit, pheasant, and game pâtés. All hard cheeses and strongly flavoured soft cheeses. Celery.

Dry white wines All hors-d'oeuvre, shellfish, lean fish, ham, breast of chicken and very delicate white meat. Mushrooms, mild soft cheeses, ice cream, melon.

Semi-dry and sweet white wines Oily fish, lobster, tripe, fried chicken, asparagus, sweet and savoury pastry dishes – and surprisingly, *foie gras*.

Note Champagne or any other dry sparkling white wine can be served throughout the meal.

INDEX